W9-COE-914

MANAGING CONFLICT CREATIVELY

A Guide For Missionaries & Christian Workers

Donald C. Palmer

WITHDRAWN
FROM THE
CARL B. YLVISAKER LIBRARY
Concordia College, Moorhead, MN

William Carey Library

PASADENA, CALIFORNIA

HD
30.29
.P35
1990
12/5/95

Copyright 1990 by Donald C. Palmer

All Rights Reserved

First printing, 1991
Second printing, 1994

No part of this publication may be reproduced, stored in a retrieval system, or transmitted in any form or by any means—electronic, mechanical, photocopy, recording, or any other—except for brief quotations embodied in critical articles or printed reviews, without prior written permission of the publisher.

Published by
WILLIAM CAREY LIBRARY
P.O. Box 40129
Pasadena, California 91114

ISBN 0-87808-231-X

Printed in the United States of America.

TABLE OF CONTENTS

I. DYNAMICS
of CONFLICT

SECTION I.

INTRODUCTION TO THE DYNAMICS OF CONFLICT

There are more people on our planet than ever before and the trend is for most of us to crowd into the major urban centers. This in itself creates the potential for greater conflicts between people. But along with this, changes are taking place so rapidly in our world that we are hard-pressed to keep up. Our fast-paced society and complex communication systems strain our coping abilities. Add to this the destructive tendencies that sin has introduced into the human race, and the result is a very volatile mixture of ingredients in human society. Out of this mixture misunderstandings, hostilities, and conflicts seem to multiply and sometimes explode.

The result of all this is that conflict is a growth industry in our day. It has existed since the beginning of human history, but its occurrence is now more frequent and its intensity greater. The increase in violence, lawsuits, and divorce in our country are all evidence of this. People once were taught to accept and submit to authority. Today we are taught to question and challenge the decisions and authority of those over us. We were taught to "turn the other cheek" but today we are encouraged to assert and defend our perceived rights. We were taught to hide our feelings and emotions and keep our composure at all times. Now it's considered far more healthy to "let it all hang out."

Besides these changes, our societies – especially the cities – are increasingly heterogeneous. The average community, school, church, and organization is composed of people from many different backgrounds, cultures, religions, races, and value systems. All of these differing viewpoints and behavior increase the likelihood of misunderstandings that in turn lead to conflicts. Churches, mission agencies, and other Christian organizations certainly are not exempt from these influences and changes.

As we study the Bible itself we find that the history of the people of God is largely a history of conflict. The New Testament reminds us that the early Christians and churches faced continual conflicts just as we do today. And church history clearly demonstrates that throughout its existence the church has faced conflicts with enemies from the outside as well as internal conflicts between church leaders and believers. The churches today are certainly no exception. Nor are mission agencies and third world churches.

Our missionaries seem to face even greater possibilities of conflict. As cross-cultural workers, they face the challenge of bridging cultural barriers and differences that can greatly increase the potential for misunderstanding and conflict. Missionaries must also maintain a number of different relationships whose interests and demands may vary greatly. They must seek to work in harmony with their sending churches, their mission agency, field leadership, fellow missionaries and national churches and leaders – all at the same time. This is no small task! One of the main reasons why so many missionaries return home is the inablity to resolve internal and interpersonal conflicts on the field.

All of this makes it essential that we understand conflict and how to manage it successfully. If we do not understand the dynamics taking place in conflict, we will tend simply to be "reactors" to whatever is happening in this process. But if we learn to understand conflict and how to work with others in managing it, we can turn it into a process for problem-solving, positive change, new goals, and relationship building. Our field leaders, missionaries, and churches need and deserve this.

In this first section we will seek to answer these questions about conflict:

- What is conflict?

- Is conflict normal and inevitable?

- Is conflict always sinful?

- What causes conflict?

- What issues need to be dealt with in conflict?

- Who is affected by conflict?

- What is the potential in conflict?

I. DEFINITION OF CONFLICT

"Conflict is a situation in which two or more human beings desire goals which they perceive as being attainable by one or the other but not by both." (Stagner, p. 136).

"Conflict occurs anytime there is a disturbance in the equilibrium and security of a protective environment." (Perry, "Church Conflict Management," p. 1).

"Conflict arises when the actions of one party threaten the values, goals, or behaviors of another party." (Shawchuck, p. 35).

"Conflict is two or more objects aggressively trying to occupy the same space at the same time...two persons each trying to have his 'own way' regarding an important decision..." (Ibid., p. 35).

Question for Group Response. From these definitions, what are some of the key ingredients in conflict?

II. THE INEVITABILITY OF CONFLICT

A. God's People have Experienced It Throughout History

1. *Conflict began with man's disobedience and fall in Genesis 3.* It will not end until the restoration of all things in eternity (Rev. 21 & 22). In the meantime we live in a world where conflict affects every dimension of our lives. This is why it is so important for us to understand the dynamics of conflict and how to manage it effectively. Jesus said, "Blessed are the peacemakers" (Mt. 5:9). As Christian leaders one of our callings is to be peacemakers in the midst of conflict.

2. *Great men of God have experienced conflict.* Men like Job, Abraham, Moses, David and Jonah in the Old Testament and Peter, James, Paul, and Barnabas in the New Testament, all experienced conflict. In fact the calling of God in their lives actually increased the amount of conflict they experienced. Sometimes they experienced conflict over issues, sometimes with other people, and sometimes with God Himself!

3. *Jesus experienced conflict and even initiated it.* When He cleansed the temple (Mt. 21:12-16), confronted the Pharisees (Mt. 23), and corrected the disciples (Mt. 8:26, Lk. 24:25-26), He was engaging in conflict. A reading of the gospels provides abundant evidence that Jesus was very confrontational when the occasion demanded it.

4. *Satan seeks to take advantage of Christians in conflict.* He does this by causing us to become discouraged and withdraw, to become angry and fight, to become stubborn and selfish so that we insist on our own way, or to become divisive and go our separate ways (not all division, however, is bad). We need to be aware of these strategies of Satan (Eph. 6:11,12). When a Christian or church is active and growing, conflict often increases because Satan then increases his opposition.

5. *God sometimes permits conflict within His will.* He does this to test us and to cause us to grow (I Cor. 11:18-19) as well as to force us to discover new and better ways of doing things (Acts 6:1-7). Sometimes we can see His purpose in allowing conflict and sometimes we cannot. But we do know that God is sovereign and that He can turn the most difficult situations into something for His glory and purpose.

B. Conflict Does Not Have To Be Bad

1. *In this life all of us will experience conflict.* Every Christian, missionary and church experiences conflict. In part this is because in spite of our best intentions, things go wrong in churches and between missionaries. All of us are very imperfect and we live in an imperfect world. Murphy's law is part of this imperfect life: "If anything can go wrong, it will."

Conflict also comes because none of us lives isolated from other persons. And in our relationships we are involved in all kinds of actions, decisions, and changes that may threaten or confuse others. If these fears and misunderstandings are not cleared up quickly, tension will mount and conflict will develop.

2. *We have to overcome the belief that all conflict is sin and therefore to be avoided.* As Christians we have a tendency either to pretend a conflict does not exist or to attribute it to a lack of spirituality. Neither of these is a realistic or helpful response to conflict. The idea that all conflict is sin is very debilitating to a group because it prevents growth, change, and new directions. It is not only impossible, but also undesirable to eliminate all conflict in the church or on the mission field.

3. *Conflict itself is not sinful.* Most conflict in itself is neither good nor bad, right nor wrong. Often it is caused by honest differences of opinion and by changes and decisions that affect people's relationships and status. Some of these will lead to conflict, but without sin. Others result not only in conflict, but also in sin.

It is the way we react to conflict that may be sinful. When disagreements and differences result in gossiping, attacking, and hurting other people, then sin has entered the conflict. The important issue is: what is our reaction and behavior in conflict? How do we deal with it?

> *"It is no sin for persons in the church to be in conflict, but often when conflicts are ignored or poorly managed, they result in sinful behavior. When conflict spills over into character assassination ('the woman made me do it'), psychological or physical destruction (as David of Uriah), lying (as Ananias and Sapphira to Peter), it is sin. Whenever love is lost to hatred, gentleness to maliciousness, truthfulness to dishonesty, humility to selfishness; it is sin. But conflict free of such behavior is not sinful. It may be scary, embarrassing and dangerous, but yet without sin"* (Shawchuck, p. 12).

III. THE UNDERLYING CAUSES OF CONFLICT

A. Territory Is Threatened Or Disputed.

Either someone is trying to infringe on or take away part of another's territory, or two or more parties are disputing the same territory. The territory threatened may be physical, psychological, or spiritual. It might affect one's relationships, material well-being, position, or values and beliefs.

1. Forms that territorial conflicts take:

- Two or more parties want to occupy the same "space" at the same time (position, ministry, privileges). The contested "space" might be a position of field leadership, a place of service, a desirable mission residence, or use of the mission jeep.

- Two or more parties propose different goals or solutions that can't all be accepted nor put into action at the same time. As missionaries many of us have witnessed or experienced strongly conflicting wishes between the Field Executive Council (FEC) and a couple regarding their placement and ministry. In such a situation both parties can't have their way.

- One party seeks to impose its decisions and goals over another party with different ideas and goals. When this happens the decisions of the stronger or more persistent party block the fulfillment of the aspirations of the other party. Unfortunately, this approach leaves the other party a loser.

2. Ways of reacting to territorial threats:

- Withdraw: "I'll take my territory away with me."
- Trade: "I'll exchange some of my territory for another."
- Share: "I'll give some away in order to protect the rest."
- Take: "I'll take another's territory by whatever means it requires."
- Redefine: "Let's draw new boundaries acceptable to all parties."

Question for Group Response. In this whole matter of "territories," why is change so threatening?

B. Expectations Are Not Fulfilled.

In our relationships we all seek to fulfil roles based on our own and others' expectations, suppositions, and agreements. Others expect certain things of us and we expect certain things of them. There are several reasons why conflict develops over expectations:

1. *Expectations are not realistic or are not clarified beforehand.*
   Sometimes we develop expectations of another person that he or she can never fulfil and this leads to disappointment and conflict for everyone involved. In missions we have sometimes tried to put round pegs in square holes. We have expected teachers to be evangelists and specialists to be church planters. In frustration missionaries have left the field with a sense of failure because our expectations were unrealistic.

   Sometimes we do not clarify expectations ahead of time. For example, a new missionary couple arrives on the field with expectations of being placed in a particular ministry and location. Field leadership has other ideas and expectations about what their ministry should be on the field, but has not made this clear to the couple beforehand. Or take the case of a local church that is changing pastors. The new pastor may come into the church with his own agenda of what he wants to accomplish in the church. The congregation, however, may have a very different agenda of priorities for him and for the church. In both of these cases the expectations of the different parties were not thoroughly discussed and clarified beforehand. The likely result? Misunderstandings and conflict develop.

2. *One party does not act according to the expectations of the other party.*
   - Marriage: differing expectations about the roles of husband and wife.
   - Family: children do not live up to parents' expectations, or vice-versa.
   - Boss-employee: what the boss wants the employee to do, is not what the employee thinks he should be doing. Or conversely, the boss fails to lead and to act according to the expectations of his employees.
   - Pastor-church: the pastor is not carrying out his ministry according to the expectations of the board, and the board is not responding and acting the way the pastor expected.

8

- Missionary-National Church: the missionary sees his/her role very differently than the national church sees it.

- Goals, schedule, budget: these have been set and agreed upon for a person or group. Performance falls far short of goals and schedule; the costs rise far above projections.

Question for Group Response; What is the key element that is so important in this whole area of expectations?

3. ***People and circumstances change.*** Everyone and everything in life experiences change. Our families change as children arrive and then grow up. Churches and institutions grow larger while others grow smaller. Older missionaries retire and younger ones arrive on the field with new ideas. Mission and church leadership changes on the field and in the homeland. Societies change along with established standards and norms. Yesterday's decisions and programs often do not meet today's needs.

All of these changes provide the occasion for conflict. Relationships between people are affected. Established territories are threatened. Expectations change for all those involved. This is why Shawchuck calls change "the seedbed of conflict"(p.36). These disruptions and intrusions create insecurities and confusion that in turn cause people to feel tension. Growing tension leads to conflict unless it is dealt with.

C. Leadership and Administration Are Faulty

1. ***Unclear relationships within the organizational structure.*** People may not be sure to whom they are responsible, who is under their supervision, or how they are to relate to their associates in other departments or ministries. Perhaps they have been asked to answer to two or more bosses at once. In the case of missionaries on the field, it may not be clear what authority the Field Director has over them, nor what responsibility missionaries have to the national church and its leaders.

2. ***Poorly defined job responsibilities.*** People in an organization (and missionaries on the field) may not understand clearly what they are supposed to do. As changes take place, job descriptions are not kept up-to-date and become farther and farther removed from reality.

3. *Breakdown of communication.* Either proper communication within the organization or group has not taken place at all, or it has not been complete nor clear. It should be a general rule that those who are expected to develop or help in a new program or ministry should be consulted during the planning stage and should receive regular and clear communication during the execution of the program.

4. *Poor Planning.* A good deal of conflict results because of a lack of planning or failure to carry through on plans that are made. People in any organization need to understand what they are aiming for, what their responsibilities are, and how they are to carry them out. The more important the enterprise, the more it deserves careful and prayerful planning aimed at effectively meeting people's needs with the best possible stewardship of resources. Where there is poor planning, people become frustrated and critical because of lack of direction and results. These negative feelings lead to conflict within the organization or group.

5. *Leadership that is too autocratic or too weak.* Under laissez-faire leadership people are left to "do their own thing" with little or no guidance and accountability. Under very autocratic leadership people have little input or authority and become demoralized and passive.

6. *Leadership that is overly political.* Some leaders deal with their staff on the basis of personal favoritism. Staff members are rewarded with special benefits, not on the basis of ability and achievement, but on the basis of personal friendship or as payback for political support. This causes low morale in the organization and conflict between staff and the leader.

D. Attitudes and Personalities Clash

1. *Prejudices and biases (conscious and subconscious).* Conflict can arise because of different perspectives about other people, especially minority groups or people who in other ways are different from ourselves. These differences might be on the basis of race, class (yuppies versus blue collar workers), background (city versus rural people), education, politics, or region (southerners versus "yankees"). Our biases and prejudices are capable of producing very strong feelings and divisions between people.

2. *Differences in temperaments, personalities, styles.* Our personality differences can really grind on others and cause conflict, especially in close relationships where people live and work with each other day after day. Some examples:

- Idealist versus pragmatist ("He has no values" versus "He has his head in the clouds").

- Impulsive versus phlegmatic (One wants to accelerate; the other wants to brake!).

- Sanguine versus perfectionist (Happy-go-lucky versus must do everything "just so").

- Organized versus disorganized (One plans ahead; the other leaves things till the last minute).

- Neat versus sloppy (Try putting these together and you will have some conflict!)

Question for Group Response. What are some of your "pet peeves" or conflict areas when it comes to others' personalities and styles of doing things?

IV. THE ISSUES INVOLVED IN CONFLICT

What kinds of things do people fight about? The answer is that we fight over just about everything. And as missionaries and in our churches we certainly do not fall behind in our creative ability to find issues to fight about! So while it would be impossible for us to give a complete list, following are the main kinds of issues over which we experience conflict:

A. Substantive Issues

1. *Conflicts over values, beliefs, traditions.* This kind of issue is one of the most serious and difficult to deal with. People are often not willing to change nor compromise on strongly held values and convictions. For Christians, and especially for those in positions of church leadership, there are issues we feel so strongly about that we are willing to fight (and even to die) for them. These are issues such as the authority of the Bible, major doctrines of our faith, purity in the church, and the practice of justice and Christian ethics in what we do.

Other value issues over which Christians have very strong disagreements are the role of women in the church, the church's position on divorce and the role of divorced people in church leadership, the exercise of the "charismatic" gifts, the "biblical" form of church government (including the role and authority of the pastor, the church board, and the congregation).

As Christians and as missionaries we also don't like to change

11

customs or traditions that we have held over a long period of time. Some of our church traditions take on the character of inspired truth that nobody must tamper with. These include issues such as the "proper" style of worship, music, and church architecture; the "proper" way of giving the invitation, of practising the Lord's Supper, of collecting the offering; the "proper" times and places for church meetings.

Question for Group Response. What are some examples of time-honored traditions (not doctrines) of your church or among your missionaries, that would be very hard to change?

2. ***Conflicts over purposes and goals.*** Normally this kind of issue is not as hard to deal with as the first, but it can still lead to very serious conflict. The issue here is: what should our mission, church or Christian organization be doing? What is our purpose, our reason for existence? And in line with that purpose, what should our goals be for a particular institution, church, team, or ministry?

Question for Group Response. Can you think of a case on your field or in your church or ministry where serious conflict developed over the issue of purpose or goals?

3. ***Conflicts over programs and methods.*** This kind of conflict is generally the least difficult to handle of the three we have mentioned so far. It has to do with the nuts and bolts of how to carry out our purpose and accomplish the goals we've established. While any kind of issue can lead to serious conflict, people are generally more willing to compromise or make adjustments on programs and methods. Here the issues have to do with:

   • How should we do it? (Strategy, methods, program).

   • Who should do it? (Organization, team).

   • When should we do it? (Schedule).

   • How much should it cost? (Budget)

4. ***Conflicts over the facts.*** Sometimes there is strong disagreement over the facts that bear upon a conflict. These are facts that answer the questions: What is happening here? How and why did the conflict start? Who is behind this and who are the persons that are involved now? Disagreement on the facts may be over issues such as:

   • The objectivity and impartiality of the one(s) seeking to uncover the facts.

- The legitimacy of the sources from which the facts have been gathered or the process used to discover them.

- The accuracy or truthfulness of the facts themselves.

5. *Conflicts over leadership.* We have already seen that poor leadership is a major cause of conflict. Here we are saying that leadership is also one of the major issues in many conflicts. In churches, the most frequent issue in serious conflict is over the pastor – his ministry, personality, leadership style, preaching and teaching ability, and his family. Half of the people in a congregation may want to "lynch" the pastor and the other half may want to "lynch" the ones who want to get rid of the pastor.

Similarly, in missionary organizations and in ministries and institutions established on the fields, some of the most serious conflicts center on leadership. And the toughest of all to handle are the ones involving a termination or change of the one in charge, especially if that person is determined to fight, by whatever means necessary, to stay in his position.

B. Emotional Issues

1. *Lack of acceptance, recognition, or appreciation.* When these are withheld from people over a period of time, it is common for those affected to become critical and to introduce conflict in order to get attention and recognition, in order to be understood by others, and in order to "get even" with the one(s) responsible. In these cases the criticisms raised are often not the real issue. The issue is that people are being ignored, used, or taken for granted.

2. *Unfair Treatment.* What a person perceives as unjust treatment may be imaginary or real, but his reactions will be the same in either case. If real it might take the form of unfair criticism, ostracism, or loss of position or status within an organization or group. One reaction to unfair treatment is to withdraw or resign. Another is to seek clarification of the situation and a restoration of one's reputation and position. But a common reaction is to fight back by criticizing and attacking the ones responsible, and by bringing others into the conflict to support one's cause.

13

V. THE FOUR TYPES OF CONFLICT

A. Intrapersonal Conflict

This is conflict within an individual. It may come as a result of inner stress caused by overwork, damaged relationships, or by family, health, or financial concerns. It may also come from feeling threatened or criticized by others at the workplace or in one's group or church. But whatever the cause, inner stress can lead to growing internal conflict that manifests itself in one of several ways:

- To blame oneself. Here a person has the feeling that his problems are due to personal failure and inadequacy. This often leads to discouragement (even depression) and withdrawal.

- To blame others. Here a person is convinced that his problems are due to having been wronged by others. He feels anger and resentment towards them and is ready to fight for his rights.

- In some cases it is not a matter of blaming oneself or others. It is rather that when people are experiencing inner stress, they are more likely to have feelings of frustration, resentment, and hostility that can erupt in conflict (over a related or unrelated issue) or aggravate a conflict that's already brewing.

Intrapersonal conflict also comes from having to choose, from among a multitude of options, how we shall live. For Christians there is both deliverance from internal conflict and introduction to a new kind of internal conflict – deliverance because we are redeemed from sin and its guilt; new conflict because we now have the struggle of two natures within (Rom. 7). This creates the constant need for the Christian to make choices that are appropriate for each situation in life. The forms this inner conflict takes might be between:

- The rational and irrational self (reality versus fantasy, especially regarding oneself).

- The temptation to sin and one's conscience.

- One's duty and one's preference for play and leisure.

- A goal one wants to achieve and the effort and discipline required to accomplish it.

- The desire to blame others for one's problems, or to accept one's own responsibility in them.

• The desire to seek glory and prosperity for oneself, or to seek first the kingdom of God and His glory.

Intrapersonal conflict can affect others in a negative way. Eventually it spills over in the group and affects personal relationships and interaction. "The person experiencing stress within is the root of conflict with others." (McSwain & Treadwell, p. 58).

B. Interpersonal Conflict

This is conflict between and among individuals. Because each person's needs, aspirations, and ways of thinking are different, there is a constant possibility for conflict due to a lack of honest communication and a lack of healthy give and take between individuals who must live and work together. And though interpersonal conflict may be over substantive issues, it is often related to differences and incompatibilities between people:

• Older versus younger (the famous "generation gap").

• Authority people versus those under them. No leader is perfect and we all experience some conflict with those over us and those under our supervision.

• Personality conflicts. Some people simply rub other people the wrong way.

• Very different backgrounds, attitudes and biases, causing individuals to see the same issue in contrasting ways.

C. Intragroup Conflict

This is conflict between members of a particular group such as a committee, team, board, faculty, or church staff. This type frequently involves conflict over substantive issues: leadership and authority, purposes and goals, programs and methods, or values and traditions. But often this type of conflict is due to distrustful relationships and a lack of open communication between members of the group.

Intragroup conflict may result because a group is hopelessly divided over an issue. Unless the conflict is resolved the group will experience lack of direction, wasted energy, and little results. Intragroup conflict may also result because a few individuals have ideas and goals that are very different from those of the organization or group and they simply cannot get excited about the direction in which the larger group is going. If the organization forces its ideas and goals on these individuals they will either become alienated and withdraw or they will stay and fight. Neither is a desired response.

D. Intergroup Conflict

This is conflict between groups within or outside of one's organization. Examples of this would be conflict between committees on the field, field leadership and the home office, the mission and the national church, or between groups within a local church or institution. Each group tends to see itself as right and to defend its turf vigorously.

Difficulties are heightened when opposing groups represent different cultures. In these cases, missionary leadership needs a good deal of cultural understanding and sensitivity as well as cross-cultural negotiation skills. In Section V of our studies we will look at some of the cultural differences that have major implications for successful conflict management in cross-cultural situations.

Our studies on conflict management will deal primarily with the last three types of conflict – interpersonal, intragroup, and intergroup. Intrapersonal conflict, of course, enters into and seriously affects the other three kinds of conflict. But a more thorough treatment of personal stress and internal conflict demands a complete study of its own.

VI. THE POTENTIAL IN CONFLICT

A. Positive Results of Conflict

> *"I am sure we can begin by agreeing that every major advance in civilization has resulted from conflict"* (Ross Stagner, quoted in Leas and Kittlaus, prologue).

1. *It is evidence of life and vitality.* There is one place in this world where you will find no conflict of any kind, and that is a cemetery. There is no conflict because there is no life there. Conflict is an evidence that people and organizations are alive! It is an evidence that people are doing creative thinking and coming up with new ideas and needed changes.

2. *It can lead to renewed motivation.* Conflict often forces us to redefine or reinforce our purpose. It forces us to make needed decisions and to take action. It requires new commitments and fresh motivation. As a consequence there is a feeling of making progress, of seeking solutions that are badly needed and perhaps overdue. People feel better about the organization or group and they feel better about their own efforts in it. There is a greater

feeling of group solidarity and group identity because together they have grappled with conflict and come out of it with shared goals and decisions.

3. *It permits the venting of frustrations.* Conflict can serve as an escape valve that allows the release of pent-up emotions and negative feelings. In many cases we have already gone a long way in successfully managing conflict when we give those involved the opportunity to freely express their concerns and frustrations. People want to feel they have been heard. If they have liberty to challenge views they do not agree with, and to argue their own case, they'll be far less frustrated and they will be more likely to stay with the organization or group they are a part of.

4. *It can lead to personal growth and maturity.* Conflict forces us to know ourselves better. It also forces us to learn how to work more effectively with others in solving problems and resolving differences. The secret is to see conflict as an opportunity for learning, personal growth, and progress in our ministries.

B. Dangers In Avoiding Conflict

1. *Needed changes are not made.* Without any conflict we tend to get into ruts (open-ended graves!) and stay there. If there is no dissatisfaction with the status quo, no constructive criticism of the way things are, no desire to change, then likely there will be little improvement and progress. Conflict forces people to look for new directions and alternatives, new strategies and programs, and better ways of relating and ministering to one another.

2. *Resentment builds up.* When an organization or group inhibits conflict, it does not cause tensions to go away. It only puts them out of effective reach. It causes members to feel less in control of the situation and increases the likelihood of an explosion of feelings and frustrations in the form of angry accusations and recriminations. The one extreme of seeking to avoid all conflict can easily lead to the other extreme of all-out war.

3. *Displacement of emotions takes place.* When conflict is avoided by those responsible at the workplace, in the church, or on the mission field, frustrations are often taken out on one's family, friends, and co-workers. Such conflict may end up hurting a lot

of innocent people unnecessarily.

4. *Discontentment, gossip, and backbiting grow.* When conflict is not managed promptly, those involved may resort to negative and unhealthy forms of dealing with the conflict and with "opponents." Ignored conflict leads to using up energy and resources on backbiting and attacking one another. These unhealthy attitudes and expressions increase the level of conflict and the agony of interpersonal hostility for those involved. They make the conflict more difficult to deal with and may leave lasting wounds even after the conflict is finally resolved.

C. Paradoxes Regarding Conflict (Leas & Kittlaus, pp. 43-48)

1. *The more people care for one another, the more likely it is they will experience conflict.* Conflict is often a function of caring. Strangers rarely fight. People who don't know and care about each other may not feel a fight is worth the effort and pain. That is why spouses, family members, and intimate friends all experience conflicts. And it is for this reason that conflict is so likely within a local church. In fact, the greater the commitment of a church's members, the greater the likelihood of conflict. Members who care deeply about their church are willing to fight for its welfare if necessary.

Question for Group Response. In this regard, are missionaries especially susceptible to conflict? Why?

2. *Failure to recognize honestly one's own motives in conflict, leads to greater levels of conflict.* When we are really in touch with our own imperfect motives and the recognition of our own flawed humanity, we become more understanding and tolerant of others and their viewpoints and actions. The one who feels, "I am totally sincere and pure in my motives, but those other people...," will be a serious obstacle to managing conflict. Nothing irritates and alienates others as much as a "holier-than-thou" attitude that leads to presenting one's case as though it were a completely pure and righteous crusade. Seldom, if ever, are our motives completely pure and we do well to recognize this when engaged in conflict.

3. *The larger the number of conflicts, the greater the stability of the organization.* This statement seems to go against logic and common sense. But what this means is that it is better to have several smaller cross-currents of conflict, than one major conflict

18

that is brewing. When there are several smaller conflicts people tend to be lining up with different people on different issues. Factions will overlap so that people find themselves joining with others in one cause, and opposing some of them in another cause. In contrast, when everyone is focused on one major conflict, they tend to become very polarized and are more likely to split into hostile factions.

CONCLUSION

The problem is not with having some conflict. As we have already seen, too little conflict in an organization may very well mean that its leaders and members are apathetic and need to be awakened and challenged. On the other hand a progressive organization that is changing to meet new demands and opportunities, will experience conflicts!

Encouraging healthy conflict and learning to deal with it openly in the early stages, fosters confidence in people's ability to face conflict and deal with it in a positive way. Those involved lose their fear of conflict, learn to over-react less in the midst of conflict, and learn to manage it rather than avoid it. The result is a more stable and healthy organization or group.

Questions – Section I.

1. *What is the main new thing you have learned about conflict in this section?*

2. *Is conflict itself sinful? When does sin enter a conflict situation?*

3. *What are the four underlying causes of conflict that we considered?*
   ....*are threatened.*
   ....*are not fulfilled.*
   ....*are faulty.*
   ....*clash.*

4. *The issues involved in conflict are either substantive or* ....
   List the five kinds of substantive issues we considered.

5. *Which kind of substantive issue is the most difficult to resolve?*

6. *What is the most common and often the nastiest issue in local church conflicts?*

7. *What are some of the positive results that can come out of conflict?*
   What are some of the dangers in avoiding conflict?

8. *Analyze each of the following cases of conflict as to: (a) Its underlying cause (b) The issue involved (c) The type of conflict (the people involved).*

> *Case #1.* The father has come home after several long days on the road. He is very tired and looks forward to an evening of quietness and rest. His son, however, needs to practice his drums for a band concert the next day. The father and son have a strong disagreement.

> *Case #2.* In a local church a significant part of the congregation, especially the younger members, want to try some new things in the worship service. They would like to use more contemporary music and instruments, experiment with drama, and change the format of the service itself. Many in the congregation, especially among the older members, are opposed to these changes. They like the worship services the way they are. Conflict is growing between the two factions.

Case #3. Instead of the church growing as everyone had hoped, attendance and membership in the church have been declining during the past year. Opinions differ greatly as to what needs to be done to turn the tide. Some feel the solution is more visitation and evangelism; others more emphasis on thorough Bible teaching; others more and better programs for the family. Some are strongly convinced that the solution is better worship and classroom facilities. The church needs to set priorities but church leaders are very divided over what really needs to be done if the church is to grow.

Case #4. Two missionary couples are working together in planting a new church. One of the men is very cautious in making decisions and wants to be sure all new efforts are well planned and budgeted for. The other missionary is very impulsive in making decisions. He goes more by "gut feelings" and is very willing to take risks. Right now the two are in conflict over purchasing a property for the new church. The cautious missionary feels the church is not ready for this move and that sufficient research has not been done on the suitability of the property. The impulsive missionary feels the church will grow in faith by taking this step and that God will somehow provide the funds. Conflict is growing between the two over this issue.

9. *Briefly describe a conflict on your field or in your church in which you are or have been involved. As you did in the above cases, analyze the conflict in regards to its underlying cause, the main issue involved, and the type of conflict it was. Also indicate what you feel would have been the likely outcome if the conflict had been avoided or ignored, and what its actual outcome was in terms of negative and positive results.*

II. STYLES of CONFLICT MANAGEMENT

SECTION II.

STYLES OF CONFLICT MANAGEMENT

There are marked differences in the way we react in the midst of conflict. Without being consciously aware of it each of us develops a pattern of behavior in conflict that reflects our background, our theology of conflict, and our past experiences with conflict. This pattern of behavior is our way of dealing with the tension that we feel in conflict. Our reactions to conflict can become so predictable that others come to expect certain patterns of behavior from us. We call these learned patterns of behavior "styles" of conflict management. In this chapter we will be considering the five major styles of managing conflict that Norman Shawchuck presents in his book "How to Manage Conflict in the Church."

Each person's style of managing conflict will vary according to the situation or the intensity of the conflict. If you are mediating a conflict as a referee, you will likely use a different style than when you are directly and emotionally involved as one of the parties in conflict. Normally you will enter a conflict using your preferred style, but as tension builds up and the situation becomes more threatening, you will move to alternate styles. We call these your "back-up" styles.

Understanding the conflict management styles will help you to consciously choose those which are most appropriate for each conflict situation. It will also help you to lead others in the use of more constructive styles of managing conflict. Consequently, in this section you will learn:

- The five conflict management styles and the characteristics of each style.

- Your own preferred and back-up styles of managing or reacting to conflict.

- The two basic concerns that affect each person's choice of styles for managing conflict.

- The style that is generally most constructive and effective in managing conflict. You will be encouraged to make this your preferred style.

- The dangers in consistently using the less desirable styles, as well as the circumstances under which it is appropriate to use them.

- The importance of learning to be flexible and intentional in your choice of styles.

I. THE FIVE STYLES OF CONFLICT MANAGEMENT

A. Avoiding (The Passive Turtle)

Motto: "I will stay out of it."

Intent: To stay out of the conflict, avoid identification with either side, be neutral. The avoider makes others take responsibility for solving the conflict. He says by his actions: "I will not stick my neck out;" "It is not my problem;" "I do not care enough about the issue to suffer tension and discomfort over it." The avoider either feels that a conflict is not worth the effort, that all conflict is wrong, or that a solution is not possible anyway. So why get involved?

Action: The avoider is unassertive and passive. He does not promote his own ideas and interests, nor helps others to promote theirs. He does not cooperate in defining the conflict, in seeking a solution, or in carrying out the decisions made. Avoiding is really a decision not to decide. The avoider's slogan might well read, "The buck passes here."

An avoider's first reaction to a conflict might be to deny that any problem exists at all. If this fails and the conflict worsens his tactic may be to withdraw and head for the nearest exit. Or it may simply be to stay on the sidelines as a silent nonparticipant in the conflict and its resolution.

Results: "You lose; I lose." Avoidance is usually a negative and non-productive strategy. The avoider abdicates all responsibility to others. Issues that are not dealt with grow and fester, leading to more serious conflict. People's energy is used up in escaping from the offending parties or the conflict issues. Paralysis may set in because of a cumulative sense of weakness and frustration. There is no risk, no trust, no growth since issues have not been grappled with and resolved. The long-term use of this style may well lead to a feeling of powerlessness, growing frustration, and deepening hostility on the part of the avoider.

When Appropriate:
- When the problem being dealt with is relatively insignificant or temporary, and when the decision will not affect long-range goals nor policy.
- When the problem really is not your responsibility. One does not have to fight every battle and it is important to learn which ones

to engage in and which ones to retreat from.

- When participants are very fragile and insecure and their level of maturity will not allow for effective management of the conflict.
- When differences are so irreconcilable that confrontation will not accomplish anything. Sometimes it may be wise to avoid certain aspects of the conflict while dealing with others.

B. Accommodating (The Lovable Teddy Bear)

Motto: "I will give in."

Intent: To preserve, at any cost, the relationships within the group and between opposing parties. The message communicated is: "Our getting along is more important than the conflict issues." The accommodator will do everything possible to reduce the risk of damaging relationsips with the others involved. Issues, goals, and progress in the work are less important than relationships.

Action: The accommodator tries to embrace everyone involved in the conflict. When confrontation cannot be avoided he will go with the proposal or solution that results in the least strain on relationships. He is assertive in seeking solutions acceptable to others, but unassertive regarding his own ideas and solutions. He often placates others by conceding his own interests and goals and by giving in to those of others. The accommodator will sacrifice himself and his aspirations and may even be willing to accept blame for the conflict if it will help to bring peace and harmony.

Results: "You win – I lose." Continued use of this style is harmful for all parties. The person who always gives in to others may begin to think less of himself and his own ideas. Eventually he will feel like a doormat. The accommodator may also come to feel that he carries on his shoulders the responsibility for maintaining good relations between members of the group. This is too heavy a load for any one person in a group to carry – it is the responsibility of all those involved.

At the same time, those who always are allowed to get their way may mistakenly begin to think that they and their ideas are superior. They will tend to become even more assertive and will expect the accommodator to give in to their goals and interests all the time. Thus they are not forced to grow because they are accustomed to getting their own way.

When Appropriate:

- As with the avoiding style, when the issue is relatively insignificant or temporary.

- When one feels unsure of his own ideas and realizes that his position is weak.

- When the long-term relationship is more important than the short-range conflict issues.

- When several equally good solutions are being considered.

C. Collaborating (The Wise Owl)

Motto: "Let's work together for everyone's good."

Intent: To achieve a "win" solution for all parties. The collaborator is both issues-orientated and relationship-orientated. He believes that people are capable of solving their problems. Conflict is not to be avoided but is to be turned into a positive, problem-solving process. This style appreciates the value of each person and places equal emphasis on each party's ideas, interests, and goals, while also seeking to maintain a good relationship between those involved.

Action: The collaborator is assertive but also flexible. He is convinced that conflict can be managed in such a way that it will lead to positive growth for both the individuals involved and the organization. He is committed to win-win decisions and promotes mutual respect, open communication, and full participation by all parties in the process of managing a conflict. By his actions the collaborator says, "I care and want to preserve relationships," but he also says, "I confront and am going to present and defend my ideas and goals as well as those of others."

The leader using this style must be firm yet sensitive to people's feelings. He will insist that all parties give clear messages as to their ideas, interests, and goals. He will guide the process of communication and decision-making in a way that ensures fairness and that avoids attacks and intimidation.

Results: "You win – I win." The collaborative style works for everybody's good. Because it encourages full participation and communication by all parties, it leads to honest clarification of issues and interests, shared decision-making, and enthusiastic implementation of agreed-upon solutions. Everyone understands what is going on and joins in problem solving. The process builds trust and stronger relationships since all parties feel important and respected. Because decisions are fully "owned" by all parties, there is a higher commitment to follow through on them. Those involved learn how to successfully manage conflict and this gives them greater confidence and know-how for managing subsequent conflicts.

When Appropriate: In the majority of conflicts this is the preferred style, especially in those involving long-term goals and relationships. Because this style aims for group consensus, it does require more time than some of the other styles. And though in the long run it is worth the extra time and effort, it may not be possible to use the collaborative style if time is very short. It also requires that participants have sufficient maturity and patience to be able to handle a process that can sometimes be risky and very demanding.

D. Compromising (The Wily Fox)

Motto: "I will meet you halfway."

Intent: To give each party some of the winnings as well as some of the losses. It follows the philosphy of give and take, of negotiating and bartering the interests and goals of each party. Since the compromiser does not feel that it is possible to satisfy everyone fully, his aim is that all parties will be at least partially satisfied, while at the same time relationships are preserved. It is a style that is very popular with politicans, collective bargainers, and international negotiators.

Action: Those using this style seek to take part of each proposal but not the whole of any of them. They use negotiation, bargaining, and trading: "We will agree to x if you agree to y." "We will give you part of what you want if you give us part of what we want." The message communicated is: "We must all submit our personal desires to serve the common good of all parties as well as the organization."

The leader using this style must be assertive but flexible in an effort to ensure that each party gets a fair share of its goals and aspirations as well as making its fair share of concessions. This style uses persuasion, and if necessary manipulation, to achieve a solution in which each party wins something. In the best of solutions it looks for a creative and effective compromise rather than a solution that simply represents the lowest common denominator.

Results: "We both win some and lose some." On the negative side, use of this style may result in watered-down solutions that are not very effective, half-hearted commitment to carry out the decisions made, and recurrence of the same conflicts but with "new faces." What appears resolved may not really be resolved. Competition between the parties may continue in more subtle ways, leading to strained relationships. Each side may expend time and energy in seeing that the other party keeps its side of the bargain.

On the positive side, though it requires partial sacrifice of all parties' interests and goals, compromise often salvages stalemates over issues and relationships. Each party gets something it wants even though it also loses something it wants. While giving up the "best," it often achieves the "good."

When Appropriate: Compromise is normally the strategy to use when collaboration fails. It is appropriate when:

- Opposing parties of equal strength are stubbornly committed to different goals and solutions.

- The goals or solutions of all parties are valid and worthwhile and the differences are not worth fighting over.

- The urgency of a rapid solution does not allow time for a thorough consideration of better solutions or a consensus decision.

- Compromise can only occur when there is something that can be divided or exchanged. This style rarely will work for resolving differences on deeply held theological convictions, values, and traditions.

E. Competing (The Aggressive Shark)

Motto: "I will get my way."

Intent: To win. This style follows the philosophy that there are only two possibilities in conflict – to win or to lose – and winning is definitely better. It isn't necessarily that the one competing wishes to hurt the other parties or damage the relationship. It is rather that he feels his own ideas, values, and goals are of supreme importance and he is willing to sacrifice relationships if necessary to achieve his goals. His attitude is, "I cannot let people stand in the way of my goals."

Action: To be assertive and, if necessary, domineering. The competitor may use smooth diplomacy or raw power, but his goal is the same: to win. He believes in give and take: "You give and I will take." In most cases he will not cooperate in finding any solution other than his own. Often he will seek to manipulate others for his cause. If necessary he will attempt to defeat those who oppose him by blocking or intimidating them. Or he may simply wear down the opposition by stubbornly insisting on his own way. The message he communicates is: "I know what is best for everyone and for the organization. My way is the only way."

Results: "I win – you lose." The long-term use of this style will result either in submission or in outright confrontation by those defeated. It often creates a polarization between the parties in conflict – a "we versus them" atmosphere. And it may leave lasting wounds that make further resolution of conflict almost impossible. The competing style also results in a lack of enthusiasm by the "losers" for carrying out solutions or goals that were forced through against their wishes. Defeated parties experience a growing sense of frustration with the way conflict has been handled and growing hostility towards the "winners."

When Appropriate:

- When a decision must be made and action taken very quickly.

- When an unpopular, but necessary decision must be made by a person in leadership.

- When a particular issue is so important to a person that his future with the organization depends on winning a decision for his cause.

- When a leader is absolutely convinced that his solution is the best and is extremely important for the organization or group. But care needs to be taken to be sure one's solution really is the best. In most cases the input of others improves goals and solutions.

II. IMPORTANT PRINCIPLES REGARDING STYLES

A. There Are Two Basic Concerns In Conflict

Whenever we are managing or involved in a conflict, we need to keep in mind that each person, consciously or subconsciously, brings one or both of the following basic concerns into that conflict.

1. *Concern for relationships.* This is a people-centered concern. Its focus is on how a conflict will affect the persons involved and their relationships. It is an extremely important concern since a local church or a group of missionaries must work in unity in order to be effective and fruitful. We do not want to sacrifice long-term relationships for short-term goals or results.

   The person who feels that people and relationships are far more important than issues and goals will usually adopt the accommodating style.

2. *Concern for issues and goals.* Here the focus is on how the conflict will affect one's own interests and goals as well as those of the organization. Effective conflict management does not depend only on reducing the amount of tension between people. It also requires dealing openly and creatively with the issues, setting worthwhile goals, making wise decisions, and furthering progress in our work and ministries.

   The person who's main concern is for issues and goals, and who has little concern for relationships, will very likely use the competing style. Those who are equally concerned for both the issues and the relationships of the people involved, will normally use the collaborating or compromising style.

B. Our Styles Can Be Changed And Modified.

Each person's present style of managing conflict has been learned by example and experience, but likely without much conscious thought. This means that each of us also has the capability of learning new styles and of consciously choosing to use the styles that are most effective and also the most fair to all parties.

As we have seen, there are attitudes and actions characteristic of each style. If we are going to change our style we must:

- Change our attitudes in terms of how we view conflict and what we want to see happen in the conflict management process.

- Make a commitment to get personally involved in seeking the best possible outcome in each conflict situation. It costs something to get involved rather than to withdraw or simply to give in.

- Ensure that our actions and behavior reflect our changed attitudes and our personal commitment to a healthy conflict management process.

C. All The Styles Have Their Appropriate Use.

As we have seen in studying the conflict management styles, each style is appropriate in certain situations. The key is for us to learn to use the appropriate style for each specific conflict. This means that we need to:

1. *Learn to be flexible and intentional in our approach to conflict.* The ideal for us is to learn to use all five of the styles, not just two or three of them. There is an appropriate time, place, and situation for using each of them. Important questions to ask are: "What will be the probable consequences of using a particular style in this situation?" "Which style best fits this conflict and will be most effective in dealing with the issues, making good decisions, and preserving relationships?"

2. *Learn to use collaboration as our preferred style.* Three of the styles – avoiding, competing, and accommodating – used only occasionally and in the right circumstances, may be appropriate and effective. But used consistently they will undermine the whole process of healthy conflict management. On the other hand when the collaborating style is used consistently it builds trust, stronger relationships, confidence in managing conflict, and positive decisions for the organization or group.

If we make a determined effort to collaborate but hit an impasse, then it is normally advisable to use a cooperative compromise approach. If this fails, it is often best to move to accommodation, then to competing or avoiding. But in adopting any of the last four styles, it is hoped that they will be used only for short-term goals and decisions and that the group will insist on collaboration for important and long-term decisions.

D. Our Back-up Styles Are Very Significant

In a persistent conflict, tensions will continue to increase. As this happens, if we see that our preferred style is not achieving what we expected, each of us will normally fall back on another style that is either less or more aggressive. Knowing what our back-up styles are will help us to anticipate how we will react as pressure builds up. Do we withdraw from the conflict or give in to the other party? Do we try to bargain, trade, or negotiate everything that is "on the table?" Or do we fight to win? Since many conflicts do become very threatening, our back-up styles are fully as significant as our preferred style in telling us what we will actually do when things get hot.

CONCLUSION:

Those of us who are engaged in ministry have a great need for growth in the styles we use in managing conflict. In a survey of two hundred church leaders, Robert Dale (pp. 80-81) found a disturbing order of preference in the styles used. Church leaders first compromised. If this did not work they then tried to avoid the differences. As a next resort they sought to accommodate to the other parties. If this did not resolve the conflict they attempted to collaborate. As a last resort they sought to resolve their differences by competing. So the order of preference was: compromise – avoid – accommodate – collaborate – compete.

Collaborating was far from being the preferred style; in fact it was next to last in preference. Compromising, a very safe and often uncreative approach, was the style preferred by most. If that approach broke down, the next reaction was to avoid or withdraw from the conflict. These are not very positive or enlightened responses. Do we fall into a similar pattern? If we do, then we definitely need to make some changes in our attitudes towards conflict and in the styles we use in seeking to manage it.

One of the major objectives in this section is that each of us will evaluate his or her present style and then will make needed changes in the way we manage conflicts in which we are personally involved.

Questions – Section II.

Questions For Small Groups

1. Indicate the style that each of the following statements describes:

    a. The first person engages in conflict in such a way as to insure that persons are not "hurt" by the conflict and relationships are not damaged...even at the expense of his own personal goals and interests, if necessary.

    b. The second person engages in conflict in such a way as to insure that his own personal goals and interests are accomplished even at the expense of the relationship, if necessary.

    c. A third person has little or no commitment to maintaining the relationship or to any personal goals in the situation.

    d. A fourth person holds a strong commitment both to maintaining the relationship and to achieving the personal goals and interest of all parties in the conflict.

    e. The fifth person is willing to bargain and negotiate the issues to whatever extent necessary to maintain relationships and at the same time to arrive at some acceptable solution, imperfect though it may be.

2. Which conflict management style is best in most conflict situations? Why?

3. Which style do you feel is next best? Why?

4. If used consistently, which styles can do the most harm to both the participants and to the long-term progress of the organization or team? Why?

5. In what sense is no management style always ideal or appropriate?

6. What are the two major concerns of participants in any conflict situation?

7. What is the significance of your back-up style(s)?

Questions For Individual Response

1. *Who becomes responsible for managing a conflict when an avoiding style is used?*

2. *When is it appropriate to use the avoiding style intentionally?*

3. *When a person uses the accommodating style, who wins in the conflict situation?*

4. *Are relationships sometimes more important than the issues in a conflict? When?*

5. *What outcome does the collaborating style seek to achieve?*

6. *When might collaborating not be the style to use?*

7. *How does the compromising style differ from the accommodating and the collaborating styles?*

8. *What is the main concern in using the compromising style?*

9. *When is it appropriate to use the compromising style?*

10. *What is the main concern of the one using the competing style?*

11. *In what situations is the competing style appropriate?*

12. *Think of conflict situations in which you have been involved most recently:*

    a. A case in which you were personally involved as one of the offended parties. What style(s) did you use?

    b. A case where you served as a third party (a referee) to help resolve the conflict. What style(s) did you use?

    c. What style do you feel you display most often? What is your primary back-up style?

    d. Ask several close associates to indicate what they feel are your preferred and back-up styles.

III. The BIBLE and CONFLICT

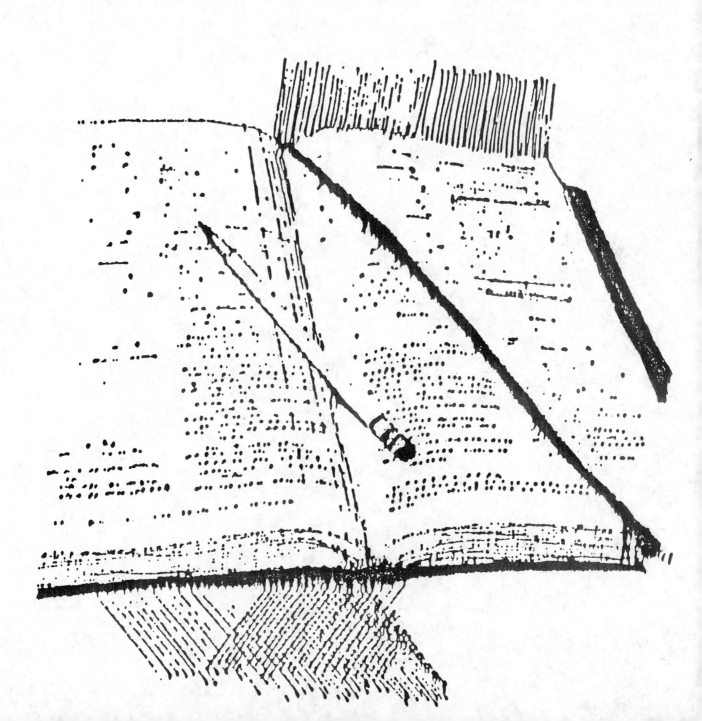

SECTION III.

THE BIBLE AND CONFLICT

The Bible tells us how conflict began, when it will end, and a great deal about how we should handle it during the interim. It makes it abundantly clear that God's people have always experienced and faced conflict. And it gives us some very informative accounts both of conflict that was well managed and of conflict that was poorly managed. We can learn a great deal from these biblical case studies.

When Adam and Eve were created there was perfect harmony on earth between man and nature and perfect communion between God and man. Man enjoyed freedom to decide and to be creative, with the only restriction being that he must not eat from the tree of the knowledge of good and evil. Man's sin of unbelief and disobedience to God's word shattered the harmony and communion that had existed. Since then conflict has entered into every part of human existence – man's relationship with God, with his fellowmen, and with creation.

The biblical record of salvation tells us about God's initiatives to restore man's relationship to Himself and to others. Yet our transformation is not perfect nor complete until we enter fully into God's presence. Meanwhile, even as Christians, we must deal with conflict as a reality that affects all of us in every aspect of life. Learning to handle conflict with His grace and wisdom is one of the greatest challenges we face in our lives and ministries.

I consider this to be an especially important chapter in this whole series of studies. First of all, because nothing has more authority than the Scriptures themselves. Then I believe that we can be most effective in teaching national leaders and churches about conflict by using biblical examples. They will likely remember more about conflict management from the Bible than from any other source. Because these biblical illustrations are so practical and so applicable for us today, they will more easily be able to apply these lessons in their own churches, ministries, and relationships.

In this chapter we will first look at a cross-section of conflicts that are recorded in the Bible. These have been classified according to the type of relationships involved. We will then study and analyze seven biblical passages that describe different kinds of conflict and how they were managed. Our objectives in this section are:

- To realize how much conflict is an integral part of the experience of God's people.

- To become aware of how frequently conflict situations are described in the Bible, and of how valuable the Scriptures are as a source of instruction in conflict management.

39

- To learn from the ways in which God's people handled conflict in different situations. We will do this by studying seven chosen passages that deal with conflict and its management.

- To learn to look at biblical accounts from the viewpoint of conflict. We have a tendency to spiritualize the Bible and to place biblical personalities on a pedestal. How could our spiritual "heroes" be involved in serious conflict? Yet as we honestly study the Scriptures we find that conflict is an important dynamic in many of the biblical accounts, and therefore is a vital key to understanding these passages.

I. TYPES OF CONFLICT IN THE BIBLE

A. Intrapersonal Conflict

- Psa. 32: David experienced conflict within himself over his sin.

- Psa. 73: Asaph experienced conflict within himself over the contradictions of life, that the wicked often prosper and the righteous often suffer.

- Mt. 27:46: Jesus experienced intense conflict within himself because he felt forsaken by the Father.

- Rom. 7:14-25: Paul experienced inner conflict because of the sin nature within him.

- Phil. 1:22-23: Paul says, "Yet what shall I choose? I do not know! I am torn between the two: I desire to depart to be with Christ, which is better by far; but it is necessary for you that I remain in the body."

B. Interpersonal Conflict

- Gen. 27: conflict between Jacob and Esau over the matter of the birthright.

- I Sam. 19: Saul feels intense conflict with David because of his jealousy of David.

- Job: a powerful account of conflict between Job and his three friends, and of conflict between Job and God.

- Amos 7:7-17: conflict between Amos, the prophet and Amaziah, priest of Bethel.

- Jonah: an extensive account of conflict between Jonah and God.

- James 4:1-3: interpersonal conflict which is due to our own wrong desires and motives.

C. Intragroup Conflict

- Gen. 37: conflict between Joseph and his brothers because of jealousy.

- Ex. 32: conflict between Moses and Israel because of the golden calf. There follows conflict between Moses and God.

- Num. 12:1-15: conflict between Moses and Aaron and Miriam because they resented his leadership.

- John 11: conflict between Jesus and the disciples as to whether they ought to return to Judea because of the danger involved (vv 7-16); followed by conflict between Jesus and Mary and Martha because he hadn't been there when Lazarus died (vv. 21-32).

- Acts 21:7-15: conflict between Paul and the believers at Caesarea over whether he ought to go to Jerusalem.

D. Intergroup Conflict

- I Kings 18: the story of dramatic conflict between Elijah and the prophets of Baal. Behind the scenes it was really a conflict between Yahweh and Baal.

- Neh. 4: conflict between those following Nehemiah and those following Sanballat and Tobiah over the project of the rebuilding of the temple.

- Mt. 21:12-16: sharp conflict between Jesus and the merchants in the temple.

- I Cor. 1:10-12 (and 3:3-4): conflict between groups in the Corinth church over leadership.

- Phil. 3:2-9 (and Gal. 5:7-12): conflict between Paul and his colleagues in ministry, and the Judaizers over the issue of keeping the law as a requirement for salvation.

II. BIBLICAL PASSAGES ON CONFLICT

In studying these passages in the light of conflict, we are well aware that the biblical personalities involved were not consciously adopting a "style" of conflict management. Nor were they necessarily aware of applying or violating good conflict management principles. For the most part they applied biblical principles to conflict, and sought to do what they felt would please God and build His kingdom. Yet these men and women used approaches and arrived at solutions that powerfully illustrate the kinds of styles and principles we are considering in these seminars.

A. Genesis 13:5-12, Abraham and Lot

Tension and conflict were growing between Abraham's herdsmen and the herdsmen of Lot because the land could no longer support the cattle of both. Abraham's and Lot's livestock operations had become so large that they and their men were now getting in each other's way and needed more land.

1. *This conflict came as a result of changing circumstances and new needs.* Contrary to what we may think, growth and prosperity themselves can often lead to conflict. In Abraham's and Lot's case, yesterday's allotment of land was not meeting their present needs. Conflict developed because both men's operations were prospering so greatly. New solutions were needed.

2. *The conflict was in its first stages and was manifesting itself in quarreling between the herdsmen.* It is important to note how Abraham reacted at this point to the conflict. He did not avoid it or pretend it did not exist. Instead he recognized the problem and sought a solution before the situation got worse. In Abraham's action we find one of the most important principles in successful conflict management: the sooner we sense a conflict is brewing and the sooner we deal with it, the quicker and more successfully we will be able to manage it. Avoiding or ignoring a conflict in its first stages is generally the surest way to have a more serious conflict on our hands.

3. *Abraham seems to have adopted an accommodating style in dealing with this conflict.* In this case he is willing to leave the outcome in the hands of God. He apparently places very high value on maintaining a good relationship with Lot and is willing to sublimate his own personal goals in order to preserve that relationship. Lot, though younger, is given the prerogative of choosing first which land he would like to have, and Abraham is willing to take what is left. Ordinarily Abraham, as the elder and the leader, would have had every right to choose first.

4. *An important cultural factor played a big part in the way this conflict was handled as well.* This cultural factor was the very strong obligation to family. Abraham, as the elder uncle, felt a great obligation to protect and watch out for his nephew, Lot. What else can explain Abraham's seemingly foolhardy action of conducting a surprise raid to rescue Lot from several powerful kings and their soldiers (Gen. 14)? In that time and culture Abraham felt he had no choice but to risk his life for his nephew.

As uncle and protector he had an obligation to Lot and he must fulfil it. Likewise as missionaries, many of you work in cultures where special obligations to family and friends will have a great influence on how conflict is handled.

B. Matthew 20:20-28, Jesus and the Disciples

The mother of James and John came to Jesus with her two sons to make a special request. She asked that Jesus promise to give the places of honor in His kingdom to her two sons. Simply put, she wanted the best for James and John and they wanted the best for themselves. In their approach they were adopting a competitive style of "we win – you lose," or at least of "we win more and you win less." We cannot be sure whether they put their mother up to making the request for them, but they certainly had someone with clout representing them. How could Jesus refuse the request of a good Jewish mother for her sons? But this is what most of us do in conflict situations. If we are not sure of the strength or popularity of our position we often look for strong allies or an effective leader that will champion our cause.

When the other ten disciples heard about it they were indignant, but not at the mother. Rather, they were angry at James and John because they were convinced that there was complicity on their part and that they were trying to take advantage of them by getting the privileged positions for themselves. After all, the other disciples would like the positions of honor for themselves, or at least they would like to keep privileges on an equal basis for all of them. They did not want James and John to get ahead of them! What we see here is a common reaction. Use of the competitive style in conflict increases the likelihood of a strong and heated reaction, if not outright confrontation.

The important lesson for us in this account is to see that conflict can be turned into a positive experience and the opportunity for learning and growth. We can see this in the way Jesus handled this conflict. The first thing He did was to take control of the situation with firmness, yet also with patience. He does not harshly reprimand James and John, nor the other ten disciples. Rather, he begins by challenging James' and John's attitudes and motivations by asking them a probing question concerning sacrifice. They were looking for special honor; Jesus talks to them about their willingness to suffer for His sake. He then turns to the whole group and uses the conflict as an opportunity to teach them two very important lessons:

1. *A lesson on the administrative structure of the Kingdom.* Jesus Himself is a servant who is under the authority of His Father. It

is the Father that will decide who will sit in the places of honor.

2. *A lesson on true greatness.* We are not called to be competitors seeking greatness and privileges for ourselves. Rather, we are called to be servants of God and of others in attitude and actions.

C. Acts 6:1-7, The Jerusalem Church and the Widows

In this conflict we again find a situation of changing circumstances. Yesterday's decisions and provisions were not meeting today's needs. The church was experiencing rapid growth and along with this the number of widows was increasing as well. The provisions of food that previously had supplied their needs, no longer were sufficient to go around. Some were being left out. What had been a very simple operation now required more administrative oversight and planning. In the midst of these deficiencies the Hellenistic Jews complained that their widows were being overlooked. A serious conflict was developing.

It is hard for us to appreciate from this brief account just how critical it was that this conflict be handled properly and with care. By its very nature it involved a very sensitive issue. If the problem was ignored and was allowed to grow into an explosion of feelings, it could drive a wedge between the Hebrew and Hellenistic Christians and even result in a permanent division between them. The situation demanded fair and decisive action. It was not a problem that would allow a very lengthy process of considering alternatives. Yet the way in which it was handled did allow everyone concerned to have a say in the decisions made.

The apostles took the initiative as soon as they became aware of the conflict. They first set clear guidelines outlining the process to be used in managing the conflict and arriving at a just solution. The apostles would oversee the process itself, while the Jerusalem believers would choose those who would oversee the food distribution program to the widows. It is a beautiful example of good conflict management. Note some of the positive aspects in this process:

1. *The apostles started by establishing priorities for their own ministry.* The church needed their leadership in the Word and in prayer. They realized that it would be a mistake for them to get sidetracked by trying to administrate this program themselves. This is a good lesson for pastors and missionaries: we should not try to carry responsibilities that will take us from our primary ministries.

44

2. *The apostles established the guidelines for the resolution of the conflict:* "Brothers, you choose seven men from among you who are known to be full of the Spirit and wisdom." The congregation was to choose seven qualified men to administrate this program and the apostles indicated what those qualifications were.

3. *The believers themselves chose the seven men.* They had "ownership" in the decisions made. Because they all participated in the process they would be more likely to accept and support the leaders chosen. We may sometimes feel that we cannot trust a congregation to make a wise decision if a choice is left to them. But here is an example of a congregation making a very wise choice that showed a great deal of Christian grace. The names of the seven men listed are all Hellenistic names. Since it was the Hellenistic Jewish widows who were being neglected, Hellenistic Jewish leaders were chosen to direct the program. This would effectively stop criticism, and the leaders appointed would feel a strong need to be very fair and impartial to both parties since they were chosen by both.

4. *There was a task orientation with a people emphasis.* A problem needed to be solved and changes needed to be made. But these were not an end in themselves; they were the means to help people who were in need while also developing people in the process itself.

5. *There were a number of short and long-range benefits from the decisive and creative management of this conflict:*

- The widows were provided for in an impartial way (implicit because the problem is not mentioned again).

- The Word of God spread in its influence (v.7).

- The church in Jerusalem experienced rapid growth (v. 7). No doubt observers admired the fairness and maturity of the church in its handling of this situation. And the world is watching us as believers to see how we handle problems and conflicts!

- New church leaders were identified and received practical training through their hands-on experience in leadership. Several of them went on to become prominent evangelists and church leaders.

- A new class of church leaders originated with the designation of these men as "deacons" (v. 1 refers to "the daily deaconing"). This new class of leaders is still blessing our churches today, almost two thousand years later!

- The believers in Jerusalem grew in their confidence and ability to solve their own problems and manage their own internal conflicts.

D. Acts 15:1-35, the Council in Jerusalem

A very serious conflict was brewing between the Judaizers and non-Judaizers. It can be seen developing in passages such as Acts 11:1-3. Here it came to a head when those of the Judaizing party came to the Antioch church and taught the recent Gentile male converts that they had to undergo the rite of circumcision in order to be saved. This resulted in "sharp dispute" (v.2, NIV) between Paul and Barnabas and the Judaizers.

Again in this case, the steps taken in the process of managing this conflict show exceptional wisdom and maturity.

1. *No parties among the Christians were left out (vv.2-5).* Paul and Barnabas could have decided to deal with the issue at Antioch and left the Jerusalem church leaders out of it. This could have had several negative results:

   - The older and more traditional group in Jerusalem would have felt slighted and ignored. But by taking the matter to the leaders of the mother church in Jerusalem they strengthened feelings of mutual respect and appreciation.

   - A division between Jewish and Gentile churches could have developed. Paul and Barnabas preserved unity by involving all parties in the Council, including the party of the circumcision.

   - Paul was still somewhat suspect by some of the leaders of the Jerusalem church. If he would have tried to resolve this conflict without them they might have concluded that Paul was an independent maverick that could not be trusted. This would have resulted in long-term damage to Paul's leadership and credibility.

2. *Proponents of opposing views were allowed to fully express their arguments and convictions (vv. 5-7a).* The major leaders did not dominate the discussion during this time of "ventilation" and airing of views.

3. *There appears to have been a fairly high level of mutual trust and respect.* The meeting did not degenerate into recriminations and each party listened to the other party's arguments.

4. *Peter, who was accepted by all parties, was the first major leader to express his convictions on the issue (vv. 7-11).* This was appropriate and very wise. What Peter said prepared the ground

for Paul's and Barnabas' presentation later on (v. 12).

5. James, the moderator of the Council and leader of the Jerusalem church, gave the wrap-up (vv. 13-21). Interestingly, he refers at this point to what Peter has said, but not Paul. No doubt this was done to bring all the parties along in the solution, since Paul was still a very controversial person.

6. The resolution of the conflict shows a combination of collaboration and compromise.

- In critical matters of the doctrine of salvation and grace, no compromise.

- In secondary matters of practice, reasonable compromise. In several sensitive matters that would offend Jewish Christians, Gentiles are instructed to respect their Jewish brothers and abstain from these practices (vv. 19-20, 28-29).

7. There was rapid and clear communication of the Council's decision to those affected by it. For best results the decisions were communicated to the churches both in writing and personally.

Resume. The council at Jerusalem was one of the most important events in the Book of Acts. Unresolved conflict and wrong decisions in that Council could have split the early Church into two opposing camps. This would have had very damaging long-term effects on all the churches, especially those made up of Gentile believers. Fortunately the wise, courageous, and collaborative management of this conflict led to a strong affirmation of the foundational Christian doctrine of salvation by grace, and to a widening door of opportunity for the Gentiles.

E. Acts 15:36-41, the Controversy Between Paul and Barnabas.

Up to this point Paul and Barnabas had worked very well together as church leaders and missionaries. Barnabas had stood with Paul as a new convert and later encouraged and promoted him for ministry in Antioch and Jerusalem (Acts 9:26-29; 12-25). They had made the first major missionary journey together. And most recently they had participated so effectively in that great church council in Jerusalem where together they defended the salvation and the inclusion of the Gentiles into the Church on the basis of grace alone. So these two men must have had a great deal of mutual respect, care, and appreciation for each other.

But now Paul and Barnabas have a very serious confrontation. Paul approaches Barnabas about making a second missionary journey. Barnabas wants to take John Mark along again. Paul does not think this is wise. The conflict over this issue is so sharp that not even their strong relationship is able to lead them to a mutual agreement. Verse 39 says tersely, "They had such a sharp disagreement that they parted company." What a sad picture! Two men who have been such close friends and effective co-workers, now split and go their separate ways.

1. *Paul and Barnabas both displayed a very competitive style in this conflict.* For Paul the success of the missionary enterprise was the most important consideration. His main concern was for the work. Paul felt strongly that John Mark had let them down when he left them to return home in the early part of the first missionary journey (13:13). He wanted someone along who could take the rigors of missionary life and who could be trained for further missionary service. Barnabas, on the other hand, wanted to give John Mark a second chance. His main concern was for a person. He probably felt that Mark's well-being and future ministry were at stake and that now, more than ever, he needed to prove himself. No doubt he felt that Mark had learned his lesson, that he was now more mature, and that he would do much better on the second missionary journey.

Both Paul and Barnabas had very strong feelings over this issue and each was determined to win his case. The conflict ended in a stand-off between these two strong-minded church leaders. Neither would give in and apparently each man felt he was right in his decision and action. In essence they were planning on two different wavelengths.

2. *There were two very important behind-the-scenes factors in this conflict.* One of them involves culture and family. Family was all important in the Jewish culture. Just as with Abraham and Lot (Gen. 13-14), Barnabas felt a duty and obligation to his nephew, Mark. Paul could be completely objective about John Mark since he had no family obligation to him, but Barnabas did not have that luxury. He probably felt he had no choice but to stand by his nephew.

The second behind-the-scenes factor at work here involves a new figure that emerges as a result of the Jerusalem Council. That man is Silas. Silas is called a leader among the Jerusalem Christians (v.22), a man who has risked his life for Christ (v.25), and a prophet and teacher (v.32). Silas had already been tried and tested and had the necessary qualities and abilities for being a good missionary partner to Paul. I personally believe that, throughout the events of Acts 15, Paul had been watching Silas and could have been thinking of him as a possible partner. Perhaps, in his mind, Paul had already made a decision about Silas before his confrontation with Barnabas about John Mark.

In any conflict, it is important to realize that the people involved come into the conflict with personal interests, obligations, and agendas. Often these are not articulated. They are behind-the-scenes factors and hidden agendas that strongly affect how people think and what they do in conflict. In managing conflict we need to seek to bring to the surface and clarify these hidden interests and cultural factors that bear upon a conflict. This requires sensitivity to people and their feelings and an understanding of the cultures represented. It also requires providing a forum for open and clear communication by all parties involved.

3. *Both men were right and both were wrong in this controversy.* Both Paul and Barnabas had valid reasons for their thinking and their decisions. But they certainly could have managed this conflict in a more positive way. For example, a compromise strategy in this situation would have called for more open discussion, less stubbornness, and greater mutual consideration of ideas and positions on the matter. Such a strategy could have sought a solution that satisfied both Barnabas' concern for Mark and Paul's concern for carrying out the missionary task as effectively as possible. Paul could have agreed to have a serious talk with Mark and, if satisfied with Mark's commitment, to take him with them on their second missionary journey. Barnabas could have agreed that if there should be a repeat of his performance on the first journey, Mark would not be invited to travel with Paul again. On the other hand, if Mark did well on the second journey, he would have proven his worth.

4. *While this conflict seems to have ended in failure, the results are very informative for us.* Even though these two very good friends and fellow workers split and went their separate ways, they lived through it and continued to be effective in their ministries. Sometimes a conflict is not resolved in what we consider to be a positive and successful way, even when a thorough and determined effort has been made. But the world does not end. Life goes on. Paul and Barnabas continued their separate ministries. Now there were two teams taking the gospel to the Gentiles and both teams had success. A new missionary leader – Silas – emerged as a result of this conflict. And John

Mark did become a disciplined and fruitful servant of God. (Col. 4:10, 2 Tim. 4:11).

The painful truth is that in some cases of conflict we are just too far apart from the other party in our ideas, convictions, or personalities. Continuing to work together just is not feasible. Sometimes the best we can do is to recognize a failed effort at conflict management and move ahead with confidence, with new associates, and with new efforts in ministry. As Paul himself said, "But one thing I do: forgetting what is behind and straining toward what is ahead, I press on toward the goal to win the prize for which God has called me" (Phil. 3:13-14, NIV).

F. Galatians 2:11-21, the Confrontation Between Paul and Peter

This was a conflict involving very basic and important doctrinal truths – salvation by grace alone, and the equality of the Gentile believers in the Church of God. But the specific cause of the conflict was Peter's actions – actions that were not consistent with the truth of the gospel. The same Peter who had overcome his prejudice when God sent him to preach to Cornelius and his household (Acts 10), and who had clearly stood for the full inclusion of Gentile believers in the Church (Acts 15), did an about face by his actions in Antioch. There Peter was accustomed to eating and fellowshipping with Gentile believers. But when Jewish Christian leaders of the party of the circumcision came from Jerusalem, Peter, fearing their criticism, drew back from the Gentile believers. Other Jewish Christians, including Barnabas, followed Peter's example. Paul felt that their actions undermined the very truth of the gospel they were preaching.

Paul decided to waste no time in challenging Peter to his face for these actions that he calls Peter's "hypocrisy"(v.13). It was a situation where compromise or accommodation on Paul's part would have been very inappropriate. And the urgency and character of this conflict excluded collaboration as the appropriate style. In this situation Paul had to be very assertive and firm. It was not that Paul had to win; it was that the truth of the gospel had to win this one. Thus Paul's competitive and confrontational style was the right one for him to use in this conflict. There are several important lessons for us from this passage:

1. *There are conflicts in which the issues are so clear and the stakes so high that we should be determined to win our case.* This is especially true in regards to important doctrinal or ethical issues. Paul's cause was right and he knew it. But we should reserve use of the competing style for those cases where we are convinced

that it is the only appropriate course to follow.

2. *Most conflicts do not fall into this category.* They usually involve issues that allow for open discussion, negotiation, and shared decisions by all parties. In these cases collaborating or compromising are the preferred styles.

3. *Paul had already established a relationship of authority and respect with his fellow church leaders.* He had earned the right to speak with authority. This "personal power base" made it possible for him to be so assertive before the other church leaders. Without his reputation as a godly leader of integrity and fairness, Paul could not have confronted Peter as he did.

4. *Paul was well prepared and his defense of the truth was thorough and powerful.* Even when we are convinced that our idea, cause, or plan is the right one, there is no substitute for being well prepared with the information, background, and facts that bear upon the issue being considered.

G. Philippians 4:2-3, the Division in the Church at Philippi.

In most of the biblical cases that we have studied so far, conflicts were recognized and dealt with in the early stages. But it appears that this was not the case with the conflict in the Philippian church. It may be that the conflict had started over an issue, but over a period of time it became focused on two major personalities. And what originally was a controversy between two capable and strong-willed women had become a conflict that affected the entire church and its witness. We can learn a great deal from the way in which Paul dealt with this serious conflict:

1. *Throughout the epistle Paul prepared the way for resolving this conflict.* The whole church must have been involved in or affected by the conflict since Paul addresses the entire congregation about its need to be like-minded and of one spirit and purpose. The apostle exhorts them to set aside selfish ambition, conceit, and self-centeredness and to learn to put first the interests and concerns of others. Apparently many of them were not doing this.

2. *Paul sought to lay a foundation of truth on which Euodia and Syntyche and their followers would have to agree.* Paul appeals to several major reasons why this conflict needed to be dealt with and resolved. It was contrary to all that it means to be Christians (2:1-4); it was completely contrary to Christ's own attitudes and actions (2:5-8); and it was a very poor testimony before the world (2:12-15).

3. *Paul does not hesitate to bring his own emotions and feelings into the controversy.* As founder of the church in Philippi he knows that he is like a father to these believers. He lets them know how much this conflict is hurting and grieving him (2:2a,16,19; 4:2).

4. *In the closing section of his letter Paul appeals directly to Euodia and Syntyche.* He openly confronts the two main parties in the conflict and exhorts them to resolve their long-standing differences. And he tells them where they can find the strength to do this difficult thing. This strength is found "in the Lord" (v.2b).

5. *Paul appoints an appropriate referee to step in as an objective third party, if necessary (v.3).* Because this conflict seems to be long-standing and deeply rooted, the two women may not be able to resolve their differences without outside help. Paul sees in this man the necessary qualifications and the proper spirit to function as a referee in this conflict. He calls him a "true yokefellow" – a peacemaker who seeks to yoke people together in unity.

CONCLUSION

It is clear that the Bible has a great deal to teach us about conflict. In the passages we have just considered we see conflict being caused by a number of factors:

- Changing circumstances that required new decisions.

- Apparent or felt injustice and favoritism.

- New and pressing needs requiring up-to-date solutions and provisions.

- Contrasting convictions regarding doctrine, traditions, and practices.

- Differences of opinion regarding people, ministries, and goals.

- Clashes of personalities and leadership.

It is also important for us to see that in all of the situations we have looked at, conflict properly managed led to new and creative solutions, some of which are still affecting and blessing us today. Well-managed conflict also resulted in:

- Deeper doctrinal convictions.
- The affirmation of important values and principles.
- A stronger testimony to the world by the Church.
- The development of new and stronger leadership.
- Clearer direction for the Church and its leaders.

Questions – Section III.

1. Abraham and Lot, Genesis 13:5-12

    a. What kind of relationship have these two men had so far?

    b. What was the cause of conflict in this situation?

    c. How was this growing conflict manifesting itself?

    d. Who took the initiative in recognizing and dealing with the conflict?

    e. What style of conflict management did Abraham reflect?

    f. Do you feel it was the right approach? Why?

    g. What were the positive results from this?

2. Jesus and the disciples, Matthew 20:20-28

    a. What caused this conflict?

    b.What motivation and "style" did James and John and their mother manifest?

    c. How did Jesus "manage" this conflict?

    d. How did Jesus use this conflict to teach and bring growth to the disciples?

3. The Jerusalem church and the widows, Acts 6:1-7

    a. What conflict situation arose in the Jerusalem church?

    b. How serious was it and what might have been the consequences if the conflict had not been managed well?

    c. Did it require a quick resolution or was there plenty of time for a lengthy study of alternative solutions?

d. What "style" of conflict management was exhibited here?

e. What part did the apostles play in resolving the conflict?
   What important consideration guided them?

f. What part did the believers play?
   How did they manifest exceptional wisdom and grace in their choices?

g. What were the positive short and long-range results in this case of successful conflict management?

4. *The Council in Jerusalem, Acts 15:1-35*

   a. What was the major issue in this conflict?
      Was this the first time this issue arose in the book of Acts?

   b. Who were the major parties in this conflict?

   c. What was the major style of conflict management reflected here and over what primary issue?
      What was the secondary style, and over what issues?

   d. What were some of the wise and positive ways in which this conflict was dealt with?

   e. What were the positive and long-term results of its successful management?

5. *The Controversy Between Paul and Barnabas, Acts 15:36-41*

   a. What kind of relationship have these two major leaders had up to this point?

   b. In their most recent involvement in conflict (vv. 1-35), how did Paul and Barnabas do?

   c. What was the conflict issue here?

   d. What was the major concern of each in this conflict?

Who do you feel was right? Wrong?

e. Do the two men appear to have taken the time and made the effort to work out a solution acceptable to everyone involved?

f. What kind of management style(s) might have preserved the relationship, and also preserved their missionary goals?

g. This conflict seems to have ended in failure. But even so, were there any positive results from it?

h. What practical lessons can we learn from this case?

6. *The Confrontation Between Paul and Peter, Gal. 2:11-21*

a. What was the cause of this conflict?

What was the major issue?

b. Did Peter know better? What motives did Paul attribute to Peter's actions?

c. What style did Paul reflect in this situation?

Would "compromise" or "accommodation" have been appropriate?

d. Why do you think Paul was successful in his very authoritative approach to this conflict?

e. In your opinion, do you feel Paul could have handled this conflict in a different or better way?

f. What lessons are there for us in our own style of conflict management?

7. *The Division in the Church at Philippi, Phil. 4:2-3*

a. What was the cause of conflict in the Philippian church?

b. What kind of women do you think these might have been?

Do you feel they each had their followers in the church?

c. How does Paul prepare the way throughout the epistle for the resolution of this conflict?

d. What would be some of the adverse results (Paul speaks to some of these in the epistle) if this conflict isn't resolved?

e. What approach does Paul first strongly propose in 4:2?

f. What other approach does he recommend in 4:3?

Why might this be necessary and what advantages do you see in this approach?

g. If this conflict is resolved successfully, what will some of the positive results be?

IV. DEVELOPMENT of CONFLICT MANAGEMENT SKILLS

SECTION IV.

DEVELOPMENT OF CONFLICT MANAGEMENT SKILLS

*"It is not the presence of conflict that causes chaos and
disaster, but the harmful and ineffective way it is
managed. It is the lack of skills in managing conflict that
leads to problems. When conflicts are skillfully managed,
they are of value" (Johnson 1978, 247).*

By now our understanding of conflict has likely been changed significantly.
We have learned about what causes conflict and whom it affects. We have
considered both its constructive and destructive potential. Hopefully we
have gained new insights into our own attitude towards conflict and the
ways in which we react to it. And we have learned valuable lessons from
Biblical accounts that describe how God's people have handled conflict in
the past.

Now in this section we are going to consider more thoroughly the
skills that we need to develop if we are to be effective conflict managers. As
we have seen, conflict is a dynamic that can either wreak great havoc or that
can lead to very positive results for an organization or group. Much
depends on the knowledge, leadership, and skills that we can bring to this
process. To aid us in developing these skills, in this chapter we will learn:

- The stages through which conflict passes as it remains unresolved
  and becomes more damaging.

- The importance of managing conflict as soon as possible, before it
  becomes more serious.

- The three essential elements in an effective conflict management
  strategy.

- The steps in the problem-solving process.

- The qualities of an effective referee/mediator.

I. LEARN THE STAGES IN THE CONFLICT CYCLE

As two or more parties try to have their own way, things are done or said
that threaten the other's territory. This causes reactions intended to protect
that territory and to set things right. This sets in motion a cycle of feelings
and behavior. As the conflict cycle progresses from one stage to another,
tension mounts and actions become more destructive.

The conflict cycle is presented by Norm Shawchuck in his workbook, "How
to Manage Conflict in the Church" (35-37). Understanding the cycle will
enable us to determine how far a conflict has developed and how intense

people's feelings are. It helps us to answer the question, "What is happening here?"

If a conflict goes on for very long, the opposing parties will begin to shift their focus away from the real issues. They will become more concerned with defending themselves and with defeating the opposing party. All kinds of peripheral issues may surface at this time. We need to try to sort all of this out. Again, an understanding of the conflict cycle will help us to do this.

- Once begun, conflict follows a five-stage progression.

- The length of time for any stage may be very short or very long, but no stage is missed.

- The conflict may be resolved at any stage.

- The further a conflict progresses, the more difficult it will be to resolve in a positive way.

A. Tension Development Stage

All conflict begins at this level. We can feel tension developing before a conflict comes out into the open, so we need to learn to listen to our senses. Tension signals that someone is feeling threatened or hurt, or is experiencing a sense of loss in some way.

At this point people are not sure what is wrong and are embarrassed to say anything because the problem seems too insignificant. But it is at this stage that conflict is best handled since there is still a measure of trust and communication, and no great harm has been done to participants.

During this stage the conflict manager needs only basic communication skills. The effective mediator will take the initiative in getting the affected parties together so they can discuss the causes of tension and how the conflict can be resolved. This involves clearing up misunderstandings and negotiating an agreement. If conflict is not handled at this stage, it will move on to the next.

B. Role Confusion Stage

Here participants are confused about what is going on and are asking: "Who and what is causing this conflict?" "Am I part of the problem?" "What should I and others be doing to resolve this?" "What is my role and what behavior is expected of me in this conflict situation?" At this stage it is extremely important that the opposing parties be talking with one another, defining:

- The issue(s) involved.

- The changes or actions that have precipitated the conflict.

- The decisions or renegotiations that need to be made to resolve the conflict.

Unfortunately, communication often breaks down at this stage because now the issues seem very threatening and the participants are uncertain about how they should relate to one another in the conflict. While initially they were embarrassed to say anything, now the opposing parties feel threatened and avoid the conflict by breaking off communication with one another.

During this stage the conflict manager will need role clarification skills. This involves the ability to help the participants in conflict to clarify their roles in starting the conflict and their responsibility for resolving it in a way that is acceptable to all parties.

C. Injustice Collecting Stage

This is the first really dangerous stage as participants begin to feel that matters can only get worse. Now the opposing parties begin to pull apart and prepare for battle. Every injustice and bad report, past or present, real or imagined, is collected to become a part of each one's artillery.

It is also the name-calling stage as each party criticizes the other as being "stubborn," "insensitive," "unreasonable," "unfair," "unspiritual and carnal." Opposing parties now expend their energies on attacking each other rather than on attacking the issues.

Since positive communication has now broken off between the opposing parties, it is vital that a mediator step in to manage the conflict. In addition to the previous skills mentioned he will need:

1. *The ability to be assertive with confidence and courage.* This involves the skill to enable opposing parties to feel on an equal basis with each other. The leader must provide a cover of protection that will allow all parties to have freedom to express their views and concerns.

2. *Spiritual authority and maturity.* At this stage a solution not only must resolve the original issue(s) but must also deal with resentments, suspicions, and harsh words and actions. The mediator may need to encourage apologies and forgiveness when these are called for. As Christian leaders we must not underestimate the importance of confession and forgiveness when conflict has become negative and destructive.

D. Confrontation Stage

This is a very sensitive and potentially volatile stage as opposing parties now confront one another. If poorly managed, each party will turn it into an occasion for justifying its own position and for blaming the other party for the conflict. It may even turn into a "fight" stage if reason is allowed to give way to anger, insults, and heated arguments.

On the other hand if confrontation is well-managed, it can become an opportunity for participants to see how damaging the conflict has become and how important it is for them to clarify and resolve their differences. During the confrontation stage the conflict mediator needs these skills:

1. *The ability to monitor and to adjust tension.* It is important for the mediator to know when to postpone and when to initiate confrontation. The latter is done by heightening tension to the point where everyone involved says, "We cannot go on this way. We have got to do something about this now."

   Here the mediator seeks to bring an unhealthy and persistent conflict to a crisis point where opponents are weary of fighting and are ready to look for a way out. Hopefully they will now be prepared to give the time and energy it will take to enter into a process for resolving their differences.

2. *The ability to keep confrontation within acceptable limits.* Lasting hurts and emotional damage can result from poorly managed confrontation. It is important for the mediator to guide the confrontation process in such a way as to avoid lasting harm to the participants or to the larger organization. This means setting guidelines as to the kind of communication and behavior allowed. It also means steering participants away from actions intended to hurt others to actions aimed at resolving the conflict.

E. Adjustments Stage

Confrontation cannot continue on forever since it taxes those involved so heavily. As a result the conflict parties look for ways to make adjustments to end the confrontation. The four main forms that adjustments can take are:

- To sever relationships with the other party. Each party goes its separate way. Missionary "casualties," church splits, divorce, and dissolved partnerships are all a result of conflict poorly managed.

- To seek to dominate the other party. The "losers" will often become passive and discouraged and will have little motivation to carry out the decisions of the dominant party.

- To attempt to return to the way things were before. But because of changes that have taken place this is seldom possible or desirable.

- To negotiate a new set of mutual agreements and commitments. This is the result of conflict well-managed.

The advantage that the conflict manager has in this stage is that the opposing parties are tired of fighting and are open to finding an agreement that will end the conflict. During this adjustments stage a skilled mediator needs:

1. *Creative thinking.* He needs to open the participants' minds to new alternatives and directions, concentrating on solutions rather than problems.

2. *Ability to gain the full participation of all parties.* The adjustments and agreements made will be successful to the extent that everyone involved has had input in them.

Resume

The key consideration in understanding the conflict cycle is that conflict is dynamic. If not managed at one stage, it will move to the next. As it does so, emotions and tension increase and the polarization of opposing parties becomes more pronounced.

If we are to be effective conflict managers we must learn to recognize in which stage a conflict finds itself, and then use the skills and strategy that are appropriate for the situation. Where we lack the necessary skills, we should seek to develop them. This chapter is intended to help us understand and develop these skills.

II. MANAGE CONFLICT IN ITS FIRST STAGES

Conflict is inevitable, and is desirable and constructive if handled properly. So we do not want to do away with conflict itself. Rather, we want to turn it into a positive process rather than a negative one. To do this, nothing is more important for us than learning to manage conflict in its early stages. If this is the only lesson we learn in this section, it will be worth it!

In medical care, especially in the third world, there has been an important shift of emphasis from "crisis" medical care to preventive medicine. In crisis care, doctors and nurses intervene when there is serious illness. But if the causes of the illness - contaminated water, lack of hygiene, malnutrition -are not dealt with, the same patients will return again and again for medical help. Preventive medicine, on the other hand, focuses on dealing with the root causes of people's health problems. The result is that they will not have to keep coming back to medical personnel for crisis care.

The same is true for conflict. We ought to place our major emphasis on dealing with it before it comes to a crisis point. In studying the conflict cycle we have seen how important it is to manage conflict in the early stages. But what can we do to promote this as a regular practice on the mission field and in our churches and Christian organizations?

A. Establish a Structure and a Philosophy Conducive to Early Conflict Management

In our missionary group, organization, or church, we need to build in structures and mechanisms that will help us to discover and deal with conflict early on. We also need to establish a philosophy and attitude that will encourage continuous and effective discussion and resolution of differences. Here are three recommendations for encouraging this process:

1. *Regular staff and membership meetings.* Missionaries and nationals working in the same ministry or area must make it a practice to meet frequently to pray about, discuss, and deal with emerging problems and issues. Some of the more serious ones will need to be passed on to field leaders for their consideration and intervention.

   In a local church there should be regular meetings of the pastoral staff, board, committees, departments, and the congregation. In any of these sessions it is important that the moderator be skilled in motivating members to "ventilate" their feelings and concerns, but with Christian respect and self control. The emphasis in any of these groups should be on the early detection and management of emerging conflict.

2. *Small groups for discussion of issues.* With large groups, such as a congregation, it may be helpful to break up into smaller groups in order to encourage broader discussion of the conflict issue(s). This way each person can be heard and have input. In some cases, each group will deal with the issue as a whole. In other cases, each group will be asked to deal with a different aspect of the larger issue and will then submit its findings and a recommendation to the larger group.

3. *Open and continuous communication as the "modus operandi"
at all levels of the organization.* The missionary, pastor, or
moderator must encourage and foster an atmosphere of freedom
and open communication for each functioning group under his
leadership. This should include:

- Opportunity for each member to point out areas of developing
  tension and to express his views and his feelings about issues and
  problems that the group is facing.

- Periodic clarification of the group's goals and plans, as well as
  clarification of expectations for each member of the group.

- Periodic adjustments of the roles and responsibilities of the
  members of the group (field missionaries, station personnel,
  church planting team, school faculty, church staff, etc.)

In Spanish there is a saying, "Arreglamos las cargas en el camino:"
"We will adjust the loads as we go along." This is what we are talking
about here. Conflict well-managed is conflict that is managed
continuously and in its early stages. It means identifying and dealing
with problems and issues as they come up in the normal process of
living, working, and planning together. Open and continuous
communication is the key!

B. Seek to Anticipate Conflict

In seeking to deal with conflict in its early stages, we need to learn
to recognize the signs of emerging conflict. What are some of the
danger signals to which we should pay special attention, and how
should we respond to them?

1. *Be alert for the following conditions that often precede conflict:*

- Someone in the group is experiencing serious problems or loss in
  his life, ministry, and relationships. Personal conflict often spills
  over into conflict with others.

- A major change is impending. Change threatens. Each one asks,
  "How will it affect me?" Often those involved react by defending
  their territory from invasion or loss.

- A longstanding problem has not been dealt with. Inaction leads to
  a build-up of pressure that can easily erupt in conflict.

2. *Note the signs of frustration that may indicate a conflict is
brewing:*

- A notable increase in complaints and criticisms by staff.

- An increase in opposition to leadership.

- Protest against the decisions, plans, or policies of the organization.

- Failure to attend meetings that are part of one's responsibilities.
- The forming of factions or opposing parties.
- A significant change in voting patterns of the group.

3. Schedule time with the parties involved for a "clear the air" session:

- Very often conflict results from misunderstandings between people and faulty perceptions of what is really going on. A session like this can dispel misunderstandings and unfounded fears.

- There may be a legitimate substantive issue at stake. Allow sufficient time for getting a clear picture of the problem and finding a good solution.

III. DEVELOP AN EFFECTIVE CONFLICT MANAGEMENT STRATEGY

The mediator must manage a conflict on three basic fronts. These involve information about the conflict, the environment in which the conflict is managed, and a proven process for problem solving. An effective strategy will deal with all three of these elements.

A. Gather the Necessary Information About the Conflict

The first step in managing a conflict is to find out what is really going on. Much of conflict is caused or aggravated by misunderstandings based on false or partial information. Consequently, it is vitally important to first get the facts and any valid information that bears upon the conflict. Some of the information may not be true or accurate, but it is valid and useful if it is perceived to be true by any of the parties involved.

1. The kinds of information needed:

- The origins of the conflict. How, why, and by whom did it start? What changes, decisions, or actions precipitated it? Who are the ones behind these decisions and changes and who are the ones affected by them?

- The substance of the conflict. What is the core issue and problem? Is the issue substantive or is it based on a personal grudge or on personality differences? Is the issue important enough to merit special effort and time?

- The emotions of the conflict. How do the people involved feel about each other personally? How much and what kind of communication is going on between them?

- The stage of the conflict. How far has the conflict progressed in the conflict cycle? If you do not intervene, what will likely happen? Do you need outside help?

- The context of the conflict. What is the past experience of the group in regards to conflict and has that experience been positive or negative? How do the parties feel about conflict itself? Are the participants mature enough to handle conflict and confrontation?

2. *Sources of valid information.* The information gathered will be only as good as its sources. Individuals who really don't know what is going on may volunteer information. The leader will be tempted to get most of his information from those with whom he feels closest and in whom he has the most confidence. But the appropriate sources of information are:

- All parties directly involved in the conflict.

- Close observers, especially those who are most impartial and objective.

- Yourself as the moderator or leader in managing the conflict.

3. *Methods for gathering information.* There are many ways to generate the information needed, depending on the stage of the conflict and the relationship between the opposing parties. The best way to get this information is from face-to-face discussion with those involved if there is still a reasonable level of communication and trust between them. In addition to this, or if open discussion between the parties is not possible, are the following methods:

- Interviews with conflict participants and with close observers. These should be carried out by the mediator or by an impartial third party.

- Small group discussions. These are especially helpful when the group involved in conflict is large, such as with a church congregation or a sizable missionary body on a particular field. Here the mediator or an impartial third party is to meet with each of the small groups to get its input on the developing conflict.

- Questionnaires. Again, these are most appropriate for a larger group where the input of many is needed but a personal interview with each person is not feasible.

4. *Sharing of the information.* Once the needed information has been gathered, the conflict mediator should call a meeting of the parties in conflict to report on his findings.

- A written report is recommended unless the conflict is simple and uncomplicated. The report should contain a categorized summary of the information that is valid and useful for managing the conflict. To make the report less formal and threatening, a blackboard, flipchart, or overhead projector can be used.

- Feedback should be encouraged. The mediator's goal is to facilitate an open discussion of the report and the opportunity to verify or modify the information shared. This gives the opposing parties their first opportunity to cooperate on a joint task that is relatively non-threatening.

- The goals in this initial meeting are: (1) to enable the parties in conflict to understand what is really going on; (2) to gain a common understanding of the underlying conflict issues; and (3) to encourage a commitment to continue the process of managing the conflict.

B. Establish a Positive Environment for Conflict Management

If a conflict is in its early stages and there is still a reasonable measure of trust and communication, intervention should be fairly simple and straightforward. Often all that is required is to get the opposing parties together for one or two sessions to clarify the issues, deal with misunderstandings and problem areas, and come to a mutual agreement on how to proceed.

But as a conflict progresses and negative emotions build, while communication and trust diminish, the task of managing the conflict becomes much more difficult. Now the mediator and the participants must deal not only with the issues, but with the whole environment of the conflict - hurt feelings, misunderstandings, fears, and anger. In order to establish an environment conducive to the effective resolution of conflict issues, the leader must first seek to:

- De-escalate the conflict by reducing the tension and negative emotions that people are feeling.

- Promote confidence, openness, and fairness during the conflict management process. How can the conflict manager do this?

1. Choose an appropriate place and time to meet. Some pointers in this regard:

- Hold meetings on neutral ground, not on either party's "private turf."

- Make sure the meeting room is pleasant, comfortable, and sufficiently large.

- Arrange for participants to sit in a semi-circle facing the moderator and the blackboard or overhead screen. This way participants are not confronting one another but are focusing on the problem together.

- Do not allow any of the parties to take a power or prestige position (head of table, raised platform, special chairs).

- Do not meet late at night when everyone is tired.

70

- Arrange for coffee breaks in order to relax and allow for informal interchange. Consider arranging for a meal together to help "break the ice."

2. *Start each session with Bible study and prayer.* We have observed that when our field leaders begin their business sessions this way, it helps to create the right atmosphere for constructive resolution of differences. When we begin a session by listening to God's Word and by asking God to lead us and to give us His blessing, we will be much less likely to fight afterwards.

Some of the Biblical passages on conflict that we considered in Section III would be especially appropriate for these studies. If there is time, allow for discussion and feedback on the passages studied. This will give the opposing parties an opportunity to share together in a positive way.

> *"Trust in the Lord with all your heart and lean not on your own understanding; in all your ways acknowledge Him and He will make your paths straight" (Prov. 3:5-6, NIV).*

3. *Project a spirit of optimism and hopefulness.* Start by giving the group reassurance about conflict itself. Point out that it is normal and that it can have a positive outcome if all parties will seek to work together on a joint solution. At the same time be careful to keep expectations in line with what is possible.

One of the biggest problems that a mediator must overcome is the fear that participants are feeling in the midst of conflict: fear of being open and misunderstood, fear of being hurt or of losing something important, and fear of alienation. An effective mediator will seek to help participants allay their fears by:

- Displaying a calm and relaxed spirit and manner. Seeing a leader who is in control will help participants to stay in control.

- Giving a clear description of what is actually happening in the conflict situation. Much of fear has to do with what is unknown or imagined.

- Presenting an understandable and sensible plan for managing the conflict.

4. *Encourage mutual trust and acceptance.* Some level of mutual trust is necessary if there is to be an openness and frankness of ideas and concerns. What can the conflict manager do to promote this?

- Make it clear that each participant has equal worth and equal say in the resolution of the conflict.

- Encourage participants to practice the "art" of listening and of "speaking the truth (but) in love."

- Emphasize that any solution will come as a result of a joint effort by all parties. No one is going to be left out in the search for an agreement that all parties can "own."

- Recognize the diversity of gifts, ministries, and personalities of those involved. Point out that conflict comes in part because individuals and groups have different motivations and priorities. Challenge each party to put itself in the other party's shoes in order to gain some appreciation of their views and concerns.

- Keep open the channels of communication. As long as all parties keep talking to one another, there is hope for a resolution of the conflict.

5. *Agree on the rules and norms to be followed.* Make it clear that failure to respect these rules and norms will only hinder the effective management of the conflict.

- It is o.k. to disagree as long as it is done with respect.

- Each person has the right to state his ideas and concerns clearly and thoroughly.

- Only one person can speak at the same time, and on one subject at a time.

- Statements must be specific and relevant to the conflict.

- Loss of temper, name calling, put downs, and attacks on another person's character will not be allowed.

- Bringing up past wrongs and mistakes unrelated to the present conflict will be discouraged.

6. *Seek to end each discussion or session on a high note.* As conflict manager, give a wrap-up that ensures a mutual understanding of the progress that the group has made up to this point. Thank participants for expressing their feelings, concerns, and ideas. Set a time for the next session and express what you hope to see accomplished in that meeting.

C. Follow a Collaborative Problem-Solving Process

Some will come into the conflict management process with their minds already made up on the conflict issues. Others come with an overly confident attitude that they have the best solutions for all problems. Others enter the process with a determination to get as little involved as possible in order to avoid any personal pain or "damage." It is a mentality that believes, "If you don't fight, you can't lose." Then there are those who see the conflict management process as a competition that they must win. Fortunately, there are also those who have a genuine desire to collaborate in finding the best joint solution possible.

How does a conflict manager avoid polarization of the group and get all parties working together on a joint agreement that will have everyone's input and commitment? In this section we will study the basic problem-solving skills that a conflict manager needs to master and follow in order to be effective.

1. *Focus on the issues.* As conflict progresses, participants often lose sight of the issue that started the conflict in the first place. They now focus attention on "the opposition" and look for new issues to rally around, many of which are unrelated to the original conflict issue. Effective conflict management requires that the mediator help participants to refocus on the original issue even while experiencing areas of disagreement.

Begin the problem-solving process by allowing time for the expression of feelings. Conflicts often do hurt. Feelings must be dealt with because they are as relevant to conflict as the facts. Consequently the conflict manager must first allow participants to express honestly how they feel about what is going on. The strategy in this stage is to work through aggressive and defensive emotions that can take over the process, so that the group can move on to the rational and productive resolution of the issues.

The more that participants share openly and honestly about their feelings and concerns, the less threatening the conflict will be. But this "ventilation" must be done within the following guidelines so that it does not become destructive for those involved:

- Each participant should express only his own feelings, not those of another.

- Participants are to respond with descriptions of their feelings, not with attacks on the other parties.

- Once feelings have been expressed and dealt with, they should cease to be the focus of the group. It is important to go beyond these to the substantive issues.

- Feelings that are expressed in these sessions should be held in confidence. They should not be shared with people who are not part of the conflict management process.

- As mediator, do not be afraid to express your own perception of what you see happening, how you feel, and what you would like to see take place as a result of this time of ventilation (i.e.: forgiveness, healing, mutual understanding and sensitivity).

Once this ventilation has taken place, the mediator should help participants to separate their personal feelings from the substantive issues. Feelings must be recognized and respected. But if we are going to resolve a conflict, we must move on to the management of the disagreements that are causing the negative feelings. The conflict manager must seek to direct participants' attention away from the persons they have been struggling with and towards the problem or issue that started the conflict.

If emotions get out of control and communication breaks down, the moderator should close off the discussion and call for a cooling off period. Then he can lead the group in analyzing what is happening and can direct the discussion back to the issues themselves.

2. *Identify areas of agreement and disagreement.* Once conflict has developed beyond the initial stages, each party tends to see itself as completely right and the other party as completely wrong. But the fact is that there are always some areas of agreement, even between opponents.

The conflict manager can build bridges of communication by first exploring these areas of agreement. When opposing groups realize that they do have some viewpoints and interests in common, they will lose some of their antagonism towards each other. Each party will see that the other side also has some worthwhile ideas. As participants experience some success in mutual problem-solving, they will be encouraged to continue their efforts to work together even in areas where there is strong disagreement.

Once areas of agreement have been identified, the next step is to identify areas of disagreement. For conflict to be managed successfully, the areas of disagreement cannot be ignored or avoided. Here is where the conflict mediator must help the parties to honestly face their differences and to search for satisfactory joint solutions. Several guidelines will help to make this a constructive process rather than a destructive one:

- Allow each party to clarify its views openly in these areas of disagreement. This will decrease the distortions that each party has about the views of the other party and may decrease the distance between them.

- Seek agreement on short-term goals as a possible step towards agreement on longer-term goals. People are more willing to give on solutions that can later be changed.

- In areas where disagreements are very strong, each party may need to work out its own independent decisions and solutions. These are then shared with the larger group for discussion and feedback.

3. *Consider possible alternatives.* As participants enter this phase in the conflict management process, there are several basic principles that, if followed, will greatly increase the possibilities for successful resolution of the conflict (Fisher & Ury 1981):

- Focus on interests, not positions. Participants must focus on meeting mutual needs, not on winning battles. To do this each party must clearly express its own interests and clearly understand the other side's interests. Then all parties should look for options that will satisfy the interests of all parties involved.

- Invent options for mutual gain. The conflict manager should seek to shift participants' thinking from "either - or" solutions (someone wins, someone loses) to the consideration of creative options that provide gains for all parties.

- Insist on using objective criteria. The strategy here is that participants make decisions on the basis of objective standards that are fair to everyone, not on the basis of which party has the strongest will and power base.

With these principles firmly in mind, the parties in conflict are ready to work on a common task: exploring possible alternatives for resolving the conflict issues. The challenge is for the group to engage in a creative search for alternatives that may be better than either party alone has thought of.

To facilitate the free flow of ideas and options, and to avoid having any party feel threatened, it is wise to separate the "idea" time from "decision" time. The best way to generate creative ideas and options is by brainstorming. In brainstorming the participants express all the ideas and alternative solutions they can think of that bear directly on the issue(s) being considered. The goal during this time of free interaction is to get a quantity of options from which the best alternatives can be chosen. For brainstorming to accomplish its purpose, the following rules should be observed:

- Participants are to seek to let go of preconceived ideas and solutions.

- All ideas are accepted; no ideas are rejected.

- No criticism of anyone's ideas is allowed.

- During this time no decisions are to be made on suggested ideas and alternatives.

- All ideas and alternatives are to be written down for later reference.

- Creativity and constructive humor are encouraged.

At the end of the "idea" phase of brainstorming, participants should begin the "decision" phase. From among the alternatives generated in the previous sessions, two or three of the best ones should be selected. It is very important that all parties be in agreement with the alternatives chosen.

If the group is still too polarized to make these choices, the conflict mediator may suggest the alternatives he feels are the best, and why he considers them so. He can then solicit feedback along with modification or confirmation of his choices by the participants.

4. *Choose the best possible solution.* This is now final decision time. From among the alternatives being considered, choose the one that all parties consider to be the best and the fairest for everyone involved. In doing this it is very important that all participants be fully involved in the decision so that they will "own" the choice that is made.

An excellent way to choose the best of possible alternatives is through use of the double column method. All parties are encouraged to come into this process with open minds and with a determination to make a joint effort at discovering the best alternative. How does this method work?

- Two columns are drawn on a blackboard, flipchart, or overhead transparency. The pros and cons are then discussed and listed for each of the alternatives being considered.

- All parties contribute their opinions and insights. As participants are involved in this process they find themselves gaining new insights and modifying their former ideas and position.

- Those who formerly were "opponents" find themselves moving closer together as they cooperate in analyzing each alternative.

- The best alternative is the one for which the positive factors most strongly outweigh the negative ones.

In using the double column method, objective criteria should be used to weigh the comparative strengths and weaknesses of the possible options. Following are some of the factors that might be considered in evaluating each alternative:

- Biblical teaching and principles. Does it meet Biblical standards?

- Good stewardship. How much will it accomplish and how many people will it help in relation to its cost?

- Its potential long-term effect on the larger group (missionary body, church, Christian organization).

- Its anticipated risks and rewards. Normally greater risks are taken only if the rewards are proportionately greater as well.

- Precedent, if it applies and is valid in the present situation.

- Resources needed for its completion - resources such as personnel, funds, materials, facilities, etc. Are they available and can the group afford them?

- The time it will take to complete in relation to the time available for meeting the need.

5. *Motivate commitment to the agreement reached.* The level of commitment that participants will give to an agreement will depend to a large extent on how well the previous steps have been followed. If all parties have participated freely in the decision-making process and the agreement made represents a true joint effort, then participants will feel personal ownership in that which they helped to create. As a result, the conflict mediator will be much more successful when he calls for a commitment by all parties to support and act on the decisions they have made.

It is important to emphasize this act of commitment in ways that will highlight its significance. Following are several recommendations for this final phase of the conflict management process:

- Put the agreement in writing. A written agreement carries more weight and may result in a firmer commitment by participants. It also reduces misunderstandings. All parties have the same information and instructions. And it serves as a continual reminder of what the parties committed themselves to do.

- Emphasize that the commitment called for is two-fold. It involves both a relational commitment (to God and to the other members of the group) and a task commitment (to the goals, plans, and strategy agreed upon by the group).

- Help "losers" save face. Even in many good agreements it is possible that some of the participants will see themselves as losing more and winning less than some of the others. Here the conflict mediator needs to discourage "winners" from gloating over their victories. Participants need to learn to win graciously. At the same time the mediator should encourage the perceived losers by emphasizing that the agreement reached, though imperfect, is better than an ongoing and destructive conflict.

77

- Celebrate the successful conclusion of the conflict. Everyone has worked hard to resolve the conflict. There have been disagreements and tensions to overcome. Now it is time for everyone to relax and celebrate. It is very appropriate to end this commitment step with a time for praise and prayer. Then consider following this with a dinner out or a time for recreation. This will help those who formerly were opponents to strengthen their relationship before getting on with the task of implementing the decisions made.

6. *Monitor and evaluate progress.* Very often this is the point at which we fail. We do not follow up on our agreements with a program of implementation and evaluation. Without this our goals and plans tend to get further removed from reality as time passes. This is because, in spite of our best intentions and efforts, our decisions and agreements are imperfect. And we live in a world where changes are constantly taking place – changes that can alter the need or effectiveness of our plans. Add to this the fact that in volunteer societies, the securing of needed personnel and resources can be especially unpredictable.

If we do not give adequate attention to following up on the agreements we have forged in conflict, we may well find ourselves back in conflict again. But this time the parties involved may be more cynical about finding a workable solution. If it did not work out this time, why should it next time? This is why it is so important to build a follow-up system into our agreements. This follow-up includes:

- Monitoring implementation of decisions made. The parties involved as well as the organization have a big stake in making the joint agreement work. To ensure this, appointed leaders need to be monitoring progress and watching for developing problems as the approved plan of action is carried out.

- Periodic evaluation of the original agreement. At agreed upon time intervals, those responsible should evaluate how the chosen plan of action is working out. As a result of this evaluation the group can: (1) continue the plan or strategy as it was originally approved; (2) continue the plan or strategy, but with adjustments and modifications; or (3) discontinue the plan or strategy if it is a failure or is falling far short of expectations. In this case those responsible may want to consider one of the other alternatives that was previously considered.

IV. THE QUALITIES AND ROLE OF A REFEREE

As missionaries, pastors, and leaders in Christian organizations we will find ourselves in situations where we will be called upon to serve as mediators in conflict. In other conflicts in which we are personally involved, we may feel it is advisable to bring in a third party to serve as referee. What are the necessary qualities to be able to function in this role?

A. He Has Confidence in His Own Worth and Abilities

The referee must believe that he can fulfil the role of mediator. This does not mean that he will always be successful. But it means that he goes into each conflict with confidence that mutually acceptable solutions are available and that he can lead the conflicting parties to a satisfactory agreement.

For a Christian, of course, there is a special confidence that comes from knowing God's Word and trusting in the Holy Spirit to guide and empower in difficult situations. This manifests itself in a deep dependence on God and on His ability to work through prayer. Confidence in God is the basis for confidence in leadership.

B. He Has the Ability to Inspire Confidence in Others

The effective leader is not just dealing in goals, strategies, and solutions; he is dealing with people. He wants to see people grow in the process of managing conflict. Speed Leas (1982, 29) writes that such a leader seeks to perform the following functions in order to keep the group healthy in the midst of conflict:

- Empower individuals to use their best efforts.

- Arouse confidence in the group's ability to manage the conflict.

- Help opposing parties to discover common goals and solutions.

- Help the group discover a strategy or process for achieving common goals and agreements.

  "Encouraging the others to join with you in dealing with the conflict and encouraging others to stay with you in the process is perhaps the single most important conflict management skill one can use" (Leas, 1092, 65).

C. He Is Flexible and Persistent

The conflict management process can take many unexpected turns, and disagreements can express themselves in various ways. The

79

mediator's first attempt to lead the conflict parties to a joint resolution may fail. Consequently, he needs to have a "second and third strike capability." If the initial approach does not work, he must be ready with contingency plans.

He must also be persistent in seeking an acceptable joint resolution to the conflict. Often the parties involved have had no training in managing conflict and may be confused, fearful, or angry. People's emotions may stand in the way of resolving the conflict. The issues involved may be difficult and complex, and solutions may come very slowly. A referee who cannot handle these frustrations and who lacks perseverance will soon become tired and discouraged, and may just give up.

D. He Does Not Take Substantive Conflict Personally

Often in conflict situations feelings can run high and words can become sharp. These may be directed at anyone involved, including the referee. He must have enough objectivity and ego strength to handle this without feeling personally threatened and without becoming defensive. In the midst of tension and disagreement he needs to be able to carry on discussion of the issues with composure and confidence.

E. He Does Not Take Sides on the Conlict Issues

A referee must be credible to all sides if he is going to be successful in leading the group to a joint resolution of conflict. Each party must see the referee as fair and impartial in representing its interests as well as those of the opposing parties.

The referee is to function as an objective third party, and as such, he should not be an advocate for the position of any of the parties involved. If, as the conflict issues are discussed, a referee finds himself taking sides, he should consider stepping aside so that an impartial referee can be brought in.

F. He Manifests Self Control and Internal Peace

Nothing will help others to maintain self control as much as seeing a leader who exercises self control. If the referee loses his patience, there is little chance that the conflicting parties will maintain theirs. The referee's ability to exercise self control in the midst of tension and disagreement is a key factor in keeping the conflict management process within reasonable and workable limits.

The referee must also experience and model peace within his own spirit if he is to be an effective peacemaker in the midst of controversy. Those involved in conflict will quickly sense and respond to what is happening within the referee himself.

> "If your own life is experiencing unresolved conflict, the conflicts of those you are trying to help will 'hook' your own conflicted spirit...The most important preparation you can make in preparing to function as a conflict manager is to prepare your own spirit." (Shawchuck 1983, 51).

1. What are the five stages in the conflict cycle?

2. Which is the most volatile stage in conflict? Why?

3. What happens if a conflict is not resolved by the time it has progressed through the entire cycle?

4. Why is it so important to manage conflict in its early stages?

5. In order to develop a pattern of managing conflict in its early stages, what two things should an organization or group do?

6. Name the three essential elements in an effective conflict management strategy.

7. What kinds of information are needed in order to understand what is happening in a conflict?

8. How should a mediator go about getting this information?

9. Once the information is gathered, what should the conflict manager do?

10. What are the two goals of a mediator in seeking to establish an appropriate environment for conflict management?

11. List the six recommendations for establishing an appropriate environment.

12. What are the six steps in the problem-solving process?

13. What is an effective method for generating as many options as possible for resolving a conflict?

14. What is an excellent method for deciding on the best of possible alternatives?

15. What determines the level of commitment that conflict participants will give to an agreement?

16. Briefly describe as many as you can of the six qualities of a referee.

Case Study In Conflict Management

(Note: in this and in subsequent case studies used in ths manual, the names of persons and places have been changed in order to protect the identity of those involved.)

Most of our Bible Institute faculty lived right on our small campus in the city of San Jose though a few of the part-time teachers lived off-campus. I was a member of our Field Executive Committee which had oversight of our missionaries on the field, including those in the Bible Institute.

Jane, one of the married teachers, had a very strong personality and was not speaking to the director of the Institute with whom she was in conflict over leadership style and school policies. It had come to the point where she avoided contact with him and with his wife, and often did not attend regular faculty or prayer meetings. This was causing a great deal of anguish for the director and his wife, who were considering resigning, partly because of this situation. The spill-over was affecting the rest of the faculty, and others outside the Institute were also becoming aware of the problem. National pastors and missionaries came to those of us on the Field Executive Committee to ask that something be done to resolve the conflict.

I felt torn because I was a friend of both the director and Doug, the husband of Jane. Yet I sympathized with the director because I felt he was doing a good job and I knew that Jane had had frequent difficulties and conflict with former directors. Those of us in leadership feared that in dealing with the conflict we could easily lose one of the couples, depending on the outcome. We felt the best solution would be one in which we could keep both faculty couples involved, yet deal with the recurring conflict and tension that Jane seemed to cause on campus. So at the next session of the Field Executive Committee we brought the matter up for discussion.

After some discussion by the FEC (Field Executive Committee), of which Jane's husband Doug was a member, we recommended that Jane and Doug continue teaching, but that they live off campus. We recognized that she was a hard-working and creative teacher, but that recurring interpersonal relationship problems were made even more serious by the fact that she lived and worked on the same small campus with most of the other faculty members. All members of the FEC agreed to this recommendation, including Doug. We felt it was a solution that would create a better atmosphere on campus as well as satisfy all parties involved. Since it was now noon, we interrupted the session and agreed to meet again after lunch.

At this point, we all felt that we had found an acceptable solution to the conflict on campus. But when Jane's husband Doug came back to the FEC meeting after having lunch with her, his former acceptance of our solution had turned into a strong determination to buck the FEC's decision and to remain on campus. Subsequently Jane and Doug enlisted supporters of their cause – especially among the nationals – to fight the FEC's decision. The FEC, however, did not reverse its decision because it realized that in doing so we could very possibly lose the Bible Institute director and his wife.

The final outcome was that Jane and Doug left the field and rationalized their cause until their departure. The whole thing caused a lot of bad feelings on the field. As for me, I felt that I lost Doug's and Jane's friendship and trust. We also discovered that some of the national leaders who had complained to us that something had to be done, were not willing later to declare themselves in this situation nor to support the decision made by the FEC.

Questions:

1. *What was the specific problem causing the conflict?*

2. *What likely would have happened if this conflict had simply been ignored?*

   What changes in attitude or behavior were necessary to really deal with this conflict? Were they dealt with?

3. *In what stage was this conflict before the FEC intervened?*

   What stage was the conflict in during the FEC's intervention?

   What was the final stage of the conflict, and what was the outcome?

4. *What style or styles of conflict management were used in dealing with this conflict?*

5. *What was the outcome of this case of conflict management? Was it successful or unsuccessful? Explain.*

6. *Several things should have been done differently in handling this conflict situation. List several of them.*

7. *What cultural factors seem to have complicated this conflict situation?*

V.
CROSS-CULTURAL FACTORS

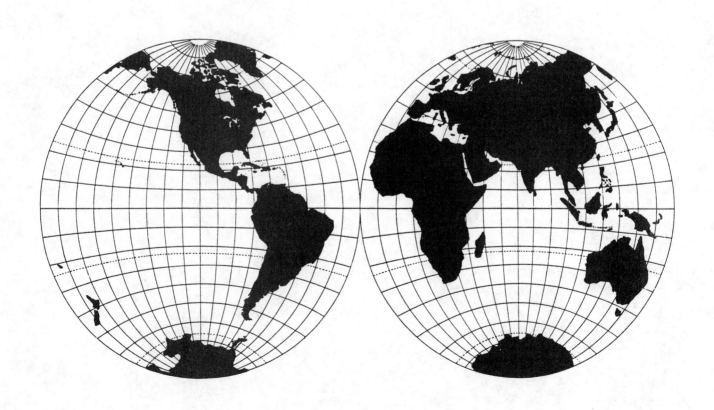

SECTION V.

CROSS CULTURAL FACTORS

Managing conflict within one's own culture can be difficult in itself. But it can be much more complicated in cross-cultural situations because of differences in language, thinking, and behavior. As North American missionaries our interests, priorities, and values are sometimes in conflict with those of our national counterparts of the host culture.

We may not understand the way nationals think and feel about conflict itself, nor the way they react and behave in the midst of conflict. For their part, they may be confused and offended by our way of resolving conflict because it is so different from the style and process they follow in dealing with it. Our failure to understand and appreciate these differences, along with an insistence on using a North American approach to managing conflict in other cultures, can only intensify and exacerbate it rather than helping to resolve it.

The importance of this is confirmed in a study by Dorothy Gish (1983, 236-242) on sources of tension for missionaries. In her research she asked more than five hundred missionaries to list and rate the principal sources of personal stress that they experienced. Nineteen sources of tension were listed by at least thirty percent of the missionaries. But the two that ranked highest were: (1) confronting others when necessary, and (2) communicating across language-cultural barriers.

So the two major areas of difficulty for missionaries were managing conflict and communicating cross-culturally. Put these together and you have cross-cultural conflict management! Fortunately we can take this as a challenge rather than an insurmountable problem. Cultural barriers can become cultural bridges as we gain understanding and sensitivity to the host culture. Missionaries who will be most successful in doing this are those who:

1. Make every effort to learn both the spoken and "silent" language of the host culture.

2. Seek to understand and appreciate the thinking, behavior, values, and interests of the nationals.

3. Are careful to behave and communicate in ways that will be understood and appreciated by their cross-cultural counterparts.

It would be impossible in this section to deal with all the cultural factors that affect conflict and its management. But I have chosen those that I feel are especially important for missionaries to understand and adapt to when involved in cross-cultural conflicts. Our objective in the study of this section is that you will gain a greater understanding of:

- The major areas of cultural difference that affect the way people view and deal with conflict.

- How we as North Americans come across to people of other cultures in the way we negotiate and manage conflict.

- Practical ideas and recommendations for negotiating and resolving conflict cross-culturally.

- Conflict analysis and problem solving through case studies in cross-cultural conflict management.

I. STYLES OF LEADERSHIP

Conflict can result when missionaries trained in a democratic/participatory style of leadership seek to manage joint ministries with nationals who practice a very different style. There are three main styles of leadership:

A. Democratic/Participatory (Voice And Vote)

The leader guides the decision-making process but all participants are free to discuss the issues and decide what should be done. Everyone's vote is equal. This is the favored leadership style in North America.

B. Consultative/Advisory (Voice But No Vote)

With this style the main leader listens to the ideas and viewpoints of participants and gets their advice. Then he makes the decision on what should be done, taking into account their input. This is a middle path between the democratic and autocratic styles.

C. Autocratic/Authoritarian (Little Voice, No Vote)

The main leader (president, chief, boss, pastor) decides what should be done and the others are to follow. Decisions can be unilateral. Participants have input only if they are asked to give it. The autocratic style is common in Africa, Latin America, and the Arab world.

Clearly, the style of leadership that is followed will affect the conflict management process. Some of the problem-solving techniques that we looked at in Section IV, would not work well in a culture that does not understand nor appreciate the democratic/participatory style of leadership and decision making. This is one of the reasons why missionaries have the hardest time adjusting to an autocractic system of leadership. Two illustrations of this style are:

1. **The "Chief" style.** On one of our African fields, the President of the Association of Evangelical Churches is a strongly authoritarian leader. In business sessions with church leaders and missionaries he may listen to what others have to say, but he has the final word. He is "the chief." This authoritarian system requires major adjustments on the part of our missionaries.

   But this leadership style follows cultural patterns. In this country each village has a chief. He is to be consulted about everything that pertains to his village and he makes the final decisions on village matters. When I visited there, each time we entered a new village, we would go first to the hut of the chief to pay our respects and discuss the purpose of our visit. It was very important that we not bypass him.

   A special problem that arises for our missionaries is that the President of the Church Association feels that he must prove to his fellow African pastors and church leaders that he really is the chief and that he is not subservient to the missionaries. So periodically he will publicly reprimand a missionary or the mission over some matter under discussion. The issue itself may be minor, but he sees it as an occasion to prove that he is really in charge. Needless to say, the missionaries on the receiving end of the reprimand do not appreciate it!

2. **The "Caudillo" style.** In Latin America the "caudillo" and "patron" system of leadership is a long-established one. Generalissimo Franco, Juan Peron, Fidel Castro, and General Pinochet are all examples of this style of autocratic and charismatic leadership. There is a great deal of power concentrated in the leader, without the checks and balances found in a democratic society.

   If autocratic leadership is responsible, fair, and compassionate, it can result in strong growth and progress for a nation, organization, or church. But it also poses the greater dangers of a repressive dictatorship, the mismanagement of resources, and an excessive personalism that makes the leader a kind of cult-hero. And in a church or ministry, there is certainly the added danger that this kind of leader will stifle the development of other effective leaders.

II. THE NEGOTIATION PROCESS

It is very important for missionaries to understand how people of the host culture view the negotiation process since this also has a significant influence on how conflict is managed in that culture. (For helpful insights on how several cultures view the negotiating process and the role of the negotiator, see Glen Fisher, "International Negotiation.")

A. Styles of Negotiation

North Americans: seek to persuade by technical competence, facts, and logical analysis. Love graphs and statistics. Generally impersonal and practical when presenting arguments. Tend to be argumentative when right or wrong. Emotions are not highly valued in negotiations. Decisions are usually made on a cost/benefit basis.

Japanese: seek to persuade through diplomacy and social interaction. Respectful and patient in negotiations. Modesty and self-restraint are highly valued. Try to persuade without confrontation. Persuasion is by a consensus-building process that can require lengthy periods of time for new proposals and major changes. Emotions are valued but must be hidden. Consequently it is often hard for westerners to understand what Japanese are thinking or feeling. The use of silence in negotiations is unnerving to North Americans who don't know what to do with long pauses without discussion.

Latin Americans: make use of power plays. To be stronger than other participants is valued. Dramatic rhetoric and style play an important part in the negotiation process. Enjoy lively interaction and debate. Emotions are highly valued and conflict interaction can be very intense. When this happens North Americans can become very uncomfortable and unsure of how they should respond.

French: seek to persuade through the use of logic, reasoning, and established standards and precedents. Prepare carefully ahead of time. Long-range decisions are very important while short-range decisions are of little consequence. Feel they have a special position and that they have no need to apologize for actions that are strictly in their own or France's self-interest. Emotions are not as important as logic and reasoning.

B. Role of the Negotiator

This has to do with how different cultures view the role of a good negotiator – the authority he carries and the style and behavior that is expected of him. To illustrate the differences we will again use the four cultures above:

North American: technical skills are valued over personal connections and relationships. Values teamwork, but each individual on a negotiating team can speak out and has room to maneuver and decide. Power games are an acceptable part of negotiation and conflict management. Confrontation and litigation are as valued as accommodation and conciliation. Has no problem mixing social occasions with business.

Japanese: age and experience are important qualifications for a negotiator. It is the group that decides, and the individual is a projection of the group he represents. Consequently the individual negotiator has very little room to maneuver and cannot change his position without consulting with his group. Americans want to know who makes decisions but the Japanese system makes this very difficult. In contrast with Americans, orientals do not appreciate discussing business issues during social occasions.

Latin American: charisma, "machismo," and good connections are important qualifications for a negotiator. The chief negotiator has a great deal of authority to make decisions, changes, and trade-offs. The key personality in the group is extremely important. Nothing will be decided until the top person in the group makes his decision. May use power plays to gain a position of strength and a personal advantage over other participants.

French: thorough training and preparation, and the official backing of one's organization or party, are qualifications for a French negotiator. Feels competent and that he represents superior logic and culture. This can irritate the other parties and causes "distancing" from them. Has no problem negotiating stubbornly in his own or his party's self interests. Not impressed by Americans' expressions of altruistic motives and intentions.

C. Place of Protocol in Negotiations

North Americans: emphasize function and downplay status and protocol. Impatient with formalities. Tend to be very casual and like to be on a first-name basis with others. This puts us at one extreme of the protocol spectrum.

Japanese: emphasize form and protocol. The status and relationship of individuals is very important. There is a proper courtesy, respect, and deference to those who are older and to those who have an equal or higher position or status.

Latin Americans: also emphasize form and protocol. Place a high value on proper form and courtesy to others in face-to-face relationships. One's social status is very important and must be given due deference. Showing proper respect for the other party's personal honor is essential and failure to do so is a serious offense (this is why dueling started!).

French: have a greater sense than North Americans do, of proper form and protocol in relationships. French society is less egalitarian than American society and more concerned about the official status and authority of those involved in negotiations.

III. TIME ORIENTATION

As North Americans we think of time in terms of specific chronological segments (months, weeks, days, hours, minutes). But in traditional cultures people generally think of time in relation to events (market day, church services, fiestas, seeding and harvest).

As North Americans we also place a very high value on time. For us, "time is money." We must not waste it or lose it. Generally our attitude is, "Let's hurry and get down to business." "We have a problem, let's deal with it." In many other cultures, however, people's attitude towards time is very different than ours.

A. Social Interaction Takes Priority

For many cultural groups, relationships and social interaction are much more important than time. It is not considered proper to rush right into discussion of issues and problems. First there are lengthy prescribed greetings, questions about family, and sharing of the latest news and matters of mutual concern. To bypass these cultural niceties would be considered rude and would hinder subsequent communication and the resolution of conflict issues.

B. Treatment of Issues Takes More Time

Negotiation, problem solving, and conflict management can take much longer in some societies than what we are used to as North Americans. Getting to the main issues may seem very slow. In the initial stage of managing conflict there is a time for carefully feeling each other out and for dealing with "safer" unrelated issues that will not cause tension or conflict. Only later in discussions, if at all, do the core issues come out.

On one of my recent trips to Ecuador, I asked our Field Director to arrange a meeting with the main leaders of the Quichua church and with our missionaries working among them. The purpose of the meeting was to discuss the opportunities and problems facing the Quichua churches and how we as a mission could best work with them in meeting needs and resolving problems. It was hoped that any areas of conflict would also be discovered and dealt with in our time together.

We met for several hours one morning. More than two hours were spent in introductions and in talking about general news and issues. Only in the last hour did we begin to get to specific issues that we felt were really important and needed to be dealt with. After the session, one of our newer missionaries expressed great frustration with the meeting, feeling it was a waste of time. He was used to getting things done quickly. On the other hand, the veteran missionary who directs our work in that area and who has worked among the Quichuas for over thirty years, felt the meeting had been worthwhile. I felt the same way. Though it had taken a long time to get to the main issues, we had communicated, had strengthened relationships, and had gotten a better idea of their thinking and concerns. Unfortunately we had not allowed enough time for fuller discussion and resolution of the major issues affecting the Quichua church and the mission.

IV. DIRECT VERSUS INDIRECT APPROACH

It is probably fair to say that in most cultures of the world, we as North Americans come across as far too direct. What we consider to be positive characteristics – openness, frankness, and honesty – may be perceived by others as rudeness and insensitivity (even in the U.S. there is a noticeable difference in directness between "northerners" and "southerners").

This distinction is especially true in the context of discussing sensitive issues or in handling serious disagreements between persons or groups. It makes conflict management between missionaries and nationals much more difficult unless missionaries have learned how to handle conflict in a way that "fits" in the host culture.

A. Way of Dealing with Disagreements

1. *Caution and diplomacy.* Where our North American approach to disagreements may be one of face-to-face confrontation and directness, the proper approach in many other cultures calls for caution, diplomacy, and indirectness.

In this regard oriental people tend to be at the opposite end of the spectrum from North Americans. They see our frankness, and what they perceive as an overbearing manner, as evidence of a lack of politeness, respect, and self-control. Because they emphasize harmony and smoothness in relationships, diplomacy is valued over directness in dealing with disagreements. On the other hand, oriental efforts to avoid giving any offense leave North Americans with little feedback and confused as to what their counterparts are really thinking and feeling. This makes it hard for us to get a "handle" on managing conflict with orientals.

Latin Americans also favor indirectness in dealing with disagreements. When speaking to a sensitive issue or an area of conflict with missionaries, they will often be so diplomatic that we as North Americans may not catch the point they are trying to make. To us they may seem to be going all around the issue rather than making their point openly and frankly. If, after repeated efforts to communicate their concerns to us in this indirect way, we do not get their message and respond to their concerns, there may be an outburst of pent-up feelings and frustrations.

2. *Saving face and preserving one's honor.* Face-saving is not as big an issue for North Americans as it is for those in many other cultures. For orientals, face-saving for everyone is very important. Decisions on conflict issues are often made on the basis of saving everyone from shame and embarrassment.

Latin Americans also prefer to handle disagreements and conflict in a way that preserves the honor and prestige of all parties, but especially of one's own personal dignity. For a Latin American, one's own honor is the most important thing in the world. A frank approach, especially if it contains anything of a critical nature, may be perceived as an attack on his honor. For this reason a careful and sensitive approach is called for in dealing with differences and managing conflict.

B. Ways of Saying "No"

There are many ways by which people of different cultures say "no" to an idea or proposal. It may be by word, gesture, or action. In their book, "Managing Intercultural Negotiations," Pierre Casse and Surinder Deol (145-46) give us seven of these ways of saying "no."

1. Silence, hesitation, lack of enthusiasm.

2. An alternative offer.

3. Postponement of a decision.

4. Blaming a third party or an outside circumstance for rejection of a proposal.

5. Avoidance of a direct response.

6. General acceptance but without any action on specifics.

7. Diverting the proponent to another idea or proposal.

In every culture a number of these ways of saying "no" are employed, but each culture varies in its preferred responses and in the frequency with which they are used. In this regard, there are several additional factors that we need to keep in mind:

- Silence may mean "no" in one culture, "maybe" in another, and tacit approval in yet another. So we need to interpret accurately what a response of silence means in a particular culture and situation.

- The use and meaning of gestures varies from culture to culture. For example, in some cultures moving the head up and down means "yes," but in others "no." In other cultures head shaking has nothing to do with agreeing or disagreeing.

- Words may give one message but non-verbal cues another. A person's words may say "yes," but his body and facial expression may say "no." We need to learn to read both verbal and non-verbal messages in the process of resolving differences.

For example, the Shuar Indians in the eastern jungle region of

Ecuador have their own way of expressing disagreement and saying "no" to a proposal. If a missionary presents an idea or plan that they are not sold on, they may agree with it publicly but take no action on it afterwards. We may ask, "Why didn't they say so when they had the opportunity?" The answer is that most of the Shuar do not want to confront or disagree publicly with a missionary whom they respect and look up to, so they give public assent to his proposal. The missionary may think, mistakenly, that this means they are in agreement with him. But their way of showing that they did not really agree with him is simply to boycott his proposal by their inaction, thus effectively nullifying it.

V. DECISION-MAKING PROCESS

This is related to the previous points but considers more specifically how people in different cultures actually make decisions. There are four principal ways in which decisions are made by an organization or group:

- Autocratically: the leader decides without consulting others.

- After consultation: the leader decides, but only after getting the input and advice of others.

- By voting: the group decides by a majority vote of participants.

- By consensus: the group decides but only when all can agree on the same solution.

In North America we favor the second and third of these approaches. We appreciate a strong and decisive leader but one who either consults with his staff before making a decision or who leads them in making a joint decision in which all have had input and vote.

In other cultures, however, we may find systems of decision-making that we are not used to. Unless we understand and adjust to these systems they can cause us a great deal of frustration and can seriously complicate the process of conflict management when both missionaries and nationals are involved.

A. Decision-Making By Consensus

This is the style that is understood and used by most orientals and by many of the agricultural indigenous societies such as the Maya, Quichua, and Aymara. Consensus by the group is the traditional way of making decisions. Cooperation, not competition nor confrontation, is the preferred approach and there is strong peer pressure to conform to group decisions. Problems and issues must be discussed thoroughly until all minds come together in one consensus decision. Glen Fisher (1980, 32) suggests that the term "direction-taking" is more descriptive of what is taking place than "decision-making." Rather than aiming for isolated and specific decisions as an end result of problem solving, the consensus system builds group direction from the beginning.

The Quichua Indians of Ecuador are an example of a people that follows a consensus method of problem solving. In each Quichua community, instead of having one strong leader, several have joint-leadership and share in decision-making. No one leader is to try to rise above the others and take authority to himself, since this would be seen as an expression of pride and arrogance. One of the leaders of a village council ("cabildo") will be named as president of the group. But he is still only a leader among equals.

This same system of decision-making that is practiced in the villages, follows over to the Quichua local churches and the Quichua Church Association. Decisions are made only after lengthy discussion and consideration of the issues has led to consensus by the group. It can be a slow process since getting everyone to agree can take a lot of time. Not even the president has a right to push through his viewpoints. All of this can be frustrating to North American missionaries who want to see things move more quickly and dealt with more decisively.

B. Decision-Making Through Strong Leaders

In Latin America we have observed another pattern of decision-making that is very different from the consensus system that we have just seen. Inherited from Spain, it is a system in which the key leader in each group effectively makes decisions for the group. In church conventions and in local churches, the decisions of members and groups often depend on what their favorite leaders decide, not on what they themselves decide.

In managing conflict this means that we have to begin the process by finding out who are the key leaders of the opposing groups. It also means that these key leaders are the ones who are going to negotiate and make most of the key decisions for their groups. Consequently they must become the focus of our efforts to resolve differences and find solutions.

C. Decision-Making Through Compromise

North Americans are enthusiastic proponents of compromise in negotiating and in managing conflict. It is our normal way of doing business and solving problems. But others may not appreciate nor use the compromising style as we do. So there is built-in conflict even in this aspect of the decision-making process.

- Orientals normally will not compromise on a decision or solution unless they can first go back to their sponsoring group for input and approval.

- The French see no reason to compromise on what they consider to be a well-reasoned and well-presented argument or position. Compromising would be appropriate only if it can be shown that their former reasoning was faulty in the first place.

- For Latin Americans, the question of whether to compromise is a matter of personal honor and dignity. Each one's concern is, "Will it reflect on my personal ability and leadership?" "By compromising, will I lose honor and respect before my friends and constituency?"

VI. PLANNING

A. Differences in the Way People Plan

People of different cultures vary greatly in terms of their experience in planning and in their understanding and approach to it. The differences are especially pronounced between articulated, formal operational societies and societies that are global and concrete relational in their thinking.

In articulated societies the different aspects of life are divided and compartmentalized. Planning in one area of life is separated from other areas of life. In global societies, however, all aspects of life are perceived as interrelated. Plans or changes that are made in one area are seen as affecting all the other areas of life as well.

Formal operational thinking is characteristic of societies with strongly developed systems of formal education and a high commitment to scientific and technological advancement. People in such societies have been taught to think in abstract terms, to hypothesize, and to plan well into the future. Concrete relational thinking is characteristic in societies that are predominantly rural and in which formal education is much more limited. Most people in these societies have not been trained in solving hypothetical problems, and are not accustomed to projecting their thinking beyond the near future.

These differences in background, education, and thinking have major implications on the way people plan, and directly affect the way they manage and resolve conflict. The kind of solutions and agreements that come out of the conflict management process will reflect these cultural patterns. As we work in other cultures, here are some of the differences that we should be aware of:

1. *Planning "while things are going on," versus summit planning.* In traditional societies people are not accustomed to setting aside special times and places for periodic and future planning. It is simply done as special needs or problems arise.

2. *Short-range versus long-range planning.* For many, planning has always been limited to the next market day, the next fiesta, or the next crop. Except in very general terms, planning for the next five to ten years is foreign to their thinking and experience.

3. *Concrete versus abstract planning.* Concrete planning deals with what can be seen and experienced whereas abstract planning deals with areas outside of one's present experience. Experimentation in new areas and ways of doing things often falls into the abstract category.

4. *Simple versus complex planning.* In many traditional societies all planning is kept simple and involves very basic and uncomplicated goals, organization, methods and programs. In technologically advanced cultures planning can be quite complex in all of these areas.

5. *Planning orientated to the present versus planning orientated to the future.* This has to do with planning that is concerned with what needs to be done right now and in the immediate future rather than at some time in the more distant future.

6. *Planning aimed at preserving traditions versus planning aimed at growth and progress.* In traditional cultures planning is committed to maintaining the status quo whereas in western societies planning anticipates and is geared to change.

7. *Planning influenced by a "limited good" view of the world versus planning influenced by an "unlimited good" view.* In a "limited good" view, some within a society can achieve greater prosperity only at the expense of others in the society. There is a limited amount of land or wealth to go around. If some get more, it means they have taken it from others who now have

less. In contrast, with an "unlimited good" view, people feel that there is enough for everyone to get ahead and become prosperous. If some have more it is not necessarily perceived as being at the expense of others. With the proper motivation and effort, everyone can get ahead. "The sky is the limit."

8. *Cautious planning aimed at lowering risks versus planning that accepts risks in anticipation of greater rewards.* In traditional and subsistence societies, people tend to be afraid of losing what little they have. "We cannot afford to try a new kind of seed. What if we lose a crop?" But in affluent societies people are in a greater position to take risks without it affecting their basic needs.

B. View of Agreements

There are important differences in the way that people of different cultures view the agreements or plans that come out of negotiation and conflict management.

1. *As serious and binding on all parties.* As North Americans we see an agreement or plan as the culmination or end point in the process of negotiation. We take agreements very seriously and cannot understand it when others do not do the same. We expect strict adherence to them, especially if they are put in writing. Because of this, some have criticized North Americans as being a contract-obsessed society.

2. *As a flexible arrangement intended to give general direction.* In contrast to North Americans, orientals see an agreement as a beginning point in the process of exploration and adaptation. As such they are resistant to agreements that are rigid and binding, and see them as an unfortunate obstacle that complicates matters. They prefer to view agreements as working guidelines that give direction but that can be easily modified and changed to fit the circumstances. When orientals do not feel the same obligation or show the same compliance to an agreement as we do as North Americans, we tend to see their actions as devious and lacking in good faith.

3. *As an "ideal" that is not really practical or binding.* Latin Americans tend to see a final written plan or agreement as a "work of art" (like a Picasso) that should be framed and hung in

its proper place. But they do not necessarily feel that it can be expected to work in the real world, so they may not follow up on it. The term for this response to elaborate and long-range plans is "proyectismo."

Most Latin Americans prefer to plan intuitively and by improvisation as needs and problems arise. They consider this to be a much more interesting, spontaneous, and creative approach to life and its problems than being bound to detailed plans and agreements that seem so restrictive. As North Americans, however, we tend to see this Latin American response to agreements and plans as indicating a lack of seriousness and commitment on their part.

TEN RECOMMENDATIONS:

In studying these cultural factors, we are not necessarily saying that certain styles or patterns are superior and the others inferior. What we are saying is that they are different. And these differences change the complexion of conflict management within each culture because they influence:

- A people's attitude towards conflict itself.

- The way a people deals with conflict issues and with the other parties in conflict.

- The outcome of a conflict in terms of the kind of agreement or results that can be expected.

If we hope to be effective in managing conflict in another culture, we must learn to adapt our approach and our expectations to fit that culture. Here are ten practical recommendations.

Learn To Be Flexible

Whenever I ask national church leaders what qualities they consider to be especially important in a missionary, one that is always mentioned is flexibility. Missionaries who are rigid in following their own cultural ways and who refuse to adapt and fit into the host culture, are not greatly appreciated. Nationals do not expect us to "go native," but they do expect us to learn and respect their ways of thinking and doing things.

This applies in the whole area of intercultural negotiations and conflict management. A stubborn adherence to our own cultural approach will only worsen a conflict. Without compromising in critical areas of faith and practice, missionaries can find ways to conform to cultural patterns and yet manage conflict effectively. In those areas in which we feel that nationals could profit from learning new approaches to conflict management, we must teach them with respect and patience, starting with key national leaders who can then teach their compatriots. The best way to begin teaching conflict management principles is to use biblical examples, as we did in Section III.

Learn To Use All Of Your Faculties

If we are going to understand our counterparts of the host culture, and communicate effectively with them, we must learn to use all of our faculties in a fuller way. This means that we must sharpen our perceptive skills in order to understand what our counterparts are thinking and why they think that way. We need to learn to observe what is really going on between people during the process of negotiation and conflict management. And we especially need to learn to "feel" what others are feeling and to express our own feelings if it is appropriate to do so.

Observing nationals who are respected and appreciated is the best way to learn appropriate behavior and reactions in dealing with conflict. The next step is to try imitating them. For example, in Latin America, try being more dramatic and showing more emotion when making a point, and see what happens. It will probably surprise them! During negotiations with orientals, use a modest and low-key approach, and practice the art of courtesy, respect, and group thinking. Try using pauses of silence (not easy for North Americans!).

Avoid Being Overly Direct

We have seen that our North American approach to negotiation and conflict management is, for the most part, very frank, analytical, and down-to-business. But because people in most cultures are less direct than we are, it is normally a wise course for us to soften our approach in dealing with conflict. We may be more direct in dealing with the issues, but we must be "soft" in dealing with the people involved. It is a matter of our learning a new style of reacting and expressing ourselves in the midst of disagreements and conflict. In Spanish, for example, the subjunctive tense of verbs, use of the reflexive, and a multitude of polite phrases, are built into the language to enable people to express themselves in a softer and less direct way. We ought to learn something from this!

We also need to learn to hear and understand when nationals are expressing criticism of our actions or disagreement with our views, even when these are expressed in a very diplomatic and indirect way. This comes by learning from the initiated and through experience.

And we must not be too quick to accept public or passive assent to our proposals as being a "yes" response on the part of the nationals. One way to guard against this as missionaries is to withhold our viewpoints and proposals until they have first given theirs. Another is to present our ideas and views through a third party who is a national (a middle man). They may feel freer to express opposition to a fellow countryman.

Keep the Pace Slow

As North American missionaries we need to learn to accept a different time orientation and to adjust our internal time clocks. This means learning patience and a willingness to "waste time" (in North American thinking) in order to achieve effective communication and problem solving.

This is not easy for us. Since we have been conditioned to see "time as money," we like to resolve differences and find solutions as quickly as possible. Once we have considered the possible alternatives we call for a decision, very often by vote. The majority "wins," but the parties involved may still be divided over the issue and the decision made.

In many cultures, however, decisions are not made until all parties agree on them by consensus. This process tests our patience since it seems very slow and indecisive to us as North Americans. But we must be careful not to rush decisions or to bypass the consensus process. It may take more time to make decisions, but once made there will be a broader base of support for them and a greater commitment to carry them out by all parties involved. In consensus cultures a unanimous decision and the preservation of relationships are of much more value than time.

Check Understanding

In cross-cultural conflict management it is vitally important to assure that mutual understanding is taking place. The conflict manager should seek to establish an internal consistency across cultural lines so that intentions, interests, meanings, and agreements are understood alike by all parties. The best way to accomplish this is by a two-way feedback process:

1. *Listen actively and acknowledge what is being said in a way that assures the other parties that you have understood them.* Paraphrase the other parties' interests and viewpoints to their

satisfaction. Ask questions and, if necessary, ask the other parties to repeat and clarify their concerns and proposals. The goal: to understand.

2. *Present your own point of view and request input from the other participants.* Anticipate that the other parties will understand what you say differently than the way you mean it. So insist on feedback and further clarify your interests. The goal: to be understood.

Be Careful About Non-Verbal Communication

What people do not feel free to express in words, may be expressed through body language. Or what is even more confusing, what is expressed in words may be contradicted by a person's non-verbal communication.

On the one hand we must learn to understand and respect the non-verbal messages that the other parties are sending. At the same time we must be careful about the non-verbal messages that we convey to the other parties. Some that may be acceptable and understood in our own culture, may be misunderstood and unacceptable in another. Some of the aspects of non-verbal communication that we must pay attention to are:

- Gestures and facial expressions
- Body language
- Space
- Eye contact
- Touch and body contact
- Tone of voice
- Clothing and grooming
- Use of silence and long pauses
- Signs of embarrassment, of being ill at ease, and of being in disagreement

Put Yourself in the Other Party's Shoes

In the process of managing conflict, we see things from our own culturally conditioned point of view and we act accordingly. But how would we feel and act if we were in the other party's shoes? To do this we must find out where the other person is coming from. This means seeking to understand his background, the problems he is facing, and the expectations others have of him. It involves a sincere effort to see the situation as the other party sees it and to feel as he feels. Understanding the other's point of view, however, does not mean having to agree with it.

We need to be especially sensitive to nationalistic feelings that may include feelings of dependency, inferiority and exploitation. Because of these feelings, national leaders from third world countries may be fearful of being seen as too cooperative with North American missionaries. In negotiating and managing conflict we must be aware of this and not expect nationals to go out on a limb before their compatriots by being overly cooperative with us. Nobody wants to be accused of being subservient to the missionaries.

Allow All Parties to "Save Face"

As we have seen, saving face is a very critical issue in many cultures. For orientals, one of the greatest stigmas is to be shamed by failing one's organization, group, or family. Meanwhile, Spaniards and Latin Americans have an almost exaggerated sense of personal dignity and honor. This personal honor must be protected at all costs. It accounts for a very strong dislike of anything that even remotely savors of criticism or failure.

Consequently, in negotiations and conflict management we should aim for creative decisions and agreements that permit all parties to save face and preserve personal honor. This does not mean giving in on important substantive issues or looking for the lowest common denominator. But it does mean being sensitive to these needs and being willing to make minor compromises and to phrase agreements and proposals in such a way that none are seen as losing.

Go Easy on Long-Range Planning

In many traditional societies people have not had the formal training nor the background and experience for complex or long-range planning. In spite of these limitations, however, there are ways in which effective planning can be done in such societies.

1. *Use short range planning (one year or less).* A long-range project or plan can be broken down into phases or steps, each of which requires less time for completion and is less complex than the whole. Rather than having to think about something that needs

to be done several years in the future, concentration is on what needs to be done in the next year or in order to complete the next step. It becomes more like "planning while things are going on."

2. *Find parallels with the kind of planning they are used to doing.* We can build upon the type of planning the people have already done in important aspects of their lives. Similar systems of planning and action can be applied to new church ministries or projects.

For example, in many traditional societies people have long used a system of volunteer help for community projects. And fiestas to celebrate special days and events have been a central part of their culture. So when we institute any new ministry, church, or project, we should consider incorporating these cultural practices in order to give the effort a big push forward and to call the attention of the community to it. Volunteers would be invited to work on the new church or project, offerings would be taken for it, and a time of celebration and fiesta would be held to initiate it. Planning that incorporates special occasions like the above is going to be especially effective in traditional cultures where people are very much event orientated.

Build an On-Going Relationship

Most conflicts between people are not one-time occurrences. This is especially true for on-going organizations and groups such as churches, missions, teams, and institutions. In all of these, relationship building should be an important goal in managing conflict. In most cases it outweighs the outcome of any one particular issue since a healthy relationship is necessary for the long-term effectiveness of any organization or group.

On the mission field relationship building is especially critical for a true partnership between church and mission. In managing church-mission conflicts, missionaries should seek to:

1. *Develop a personal relationship with national counterparts before the conflict management process begins.*

2. *Resolve differences in a way that will help future relations rather than hinder them.*

3. If necessary, give in rather than fight on issues or proposals that are of secondary importance or that have only short-range significance. This does not mean giving in to nationals in every conflict nor does it mean compromising on important principles and issues. There are times when as missionaries we will have to be firm and negotiate "hard." But we can negotiate hard and still be soft on people by being sensitive to their interests and concerns, by treating them as equals, and by resolving differences with fairness and respect.

CONCLUSION:

In this series of studies we have looked at conflict in a way that may be new for many of you. We have seen that skillful management of conflict is essential to healthy ministries, relationships, and organizational life. To this end we have looked at ways in which we can develop our skills and effectiveness in managing and mediating conflict.

Now in this final section we have considered some of the major cultural differences that affect a society's view of conflict and its way of managing it. We have also considered a number of recommendations for bridging the cultural gap and resolving cross-cultural conflict successfully.

These studies are intended to serve as an introduction to this important subject. I encourage you to continue your study of conflict management so that you might further develop your understanding and skills in this sensitive area of ministry.

> *"The optimum situation...is not the absence of conflict,*
> *a situation where the church is apathetic and lacking in*
> *creativity, nor is it the situation where persons are*
> *continually bickering, and fighting, and attacking.*
> *Rather, conflict well used and managed is present and*
> *is handled to energize and mobilize the people to initiate*
> *action and respond to needs that they really care about*
> *in the church and its community." (Leas and Kittlaus*
> *1973, 38).*

Questions – Section V

1. *In Dorothy Gish's study on sources of tension for missionaries, what were the two that gave them the greatest amount of personal stress?*

2. *What are the three major styles of leadership and which of these is the preferred style in North America?*

   How do these styles influence the way conflict is managed?

3. *What are the major characteristics in the negotiating styles of:*

   North Americans

   Japanese

   Latin Americans

   French

4. *How does a society's time orientation affect the resolution of conflict?*

5. *In terms of a direct or indirect approach to resolving differences, how are North Americans perceived in many other cultures?*

6. *What kinds of decision-making might cause special frustration for North American missionaries? Why?*

7. *List as many as you can of the differences in the way people plan.*

   How do these differences affect conflict management?

8. *What are some of the ways in which people of different cultures say "no"?*

   How do these affect conflict management?

9. *What cultural differences are there in the way people view written agreements?*

10. *List as many as you can of the ten recommendations given for managing cross-cultural conflict more effectively.*

Case Study No. 1

In Peru, South America, communication had broken down between Bob, one of our missionaries, and Carlos, a gifted Peruvian leader. Bob was involved in basic evangelism and church planting while Carlos was director of radio ministries. Both of the men are well-educated and have strong leadership abilities. The original conflict issue involved the use of mission funds for major capital improvements of the radio station as well as the purchase of new equipment for the recording studio. Bob felt that the radio ministry was not a top priority for the use of mission funds and that other programs should rate higher, such as urban church planting and the training of national leaders. Carlos, the director of radio ministries, was aware of Bob's viewpoint on this and did not appreciate it. A conflict developed over this issue and resulted in a strained relationship and the breakdown of communication between them. They were now avoiding each other.

Dave, our field director in Peru, asked Bob and Carlos to meet with him one evening after a Bible study for professional people. He felt that the best way to handle this was to bring the two men together, get the issue out in the open, and discuss it in a frank and open manner. Dave was fairly comfortable and optimistic in serving as a neutral party because he appreciated and felt confidence with both men. His main concern was whether Carlos and Bob would recognize the growing conflict between them and would be willing to be open with each other. Dave hoped that the three of them could come to a mutually acceptable understanding on priorities for the use of mission funds. If they did not succeed in this, he hoped that while Carlos and Bob might continue to disagree on what they considered to be ministry priorities, they would at least reestablish an open relationship and communication.

Dave first asked that they discuss the conflict issue itself, with each man having freedom to express his point of view. He brought out that each of the men's training, motivation, and present ministry led them to different priorities, but that they should look at how their different ministries could work together to accomplish mutual goals. He also emphasized that even though Bob and Carlos had different points of view, this should not lead to a loss of fellowship or communication between them. They could "agree to disagree."

Dave was hoping that the three of them could work together in resolving the conflict in the best way for all parties, regarding both the issue involved and the relationship. He wanted to see a win-win solution. Both of the men were encouraged to express themselves and suggest possible solutions. Dave had a strong feeling during and after the session that both men came to more fully understand the other's point of view. There was a determination to see how the radio ministry could make a greater contribution in evangelism, the development of churches, and the training of national leaders. At the same time they discussed how the radio ministry had already helped the churches and the cause of Christ by breaking down barriers and presenting a positive witness for the evangelical cause in the cities where our programs were aired.

Dave felt good about the session and so did our missionary, Bob. Both he and Carlos had come to a much better acceptance of the other's point of view. Fellowship and communication were restored. For a time, however, Carlos seemed somewhat put out with Dave for having initiated such a frank, face-to-face discussion about such a sensitive issue. This direct approach to managing conflict made him feel very uncomfortable. But after Dave had visited with Carlos several times during the coming weeks, everything seemed fine between them again.

Questions:

1. *What was the real and underlying issue in this conflict?*

2. *At what stage was this conflict in the conflict cycle?*

3. *What might have been some of the likely outcomes if this conflict hadn't been dealt with?*

4. *What was lacking between Bob and Carlos that heightened the conflict?*

5. *What style of conflict management did the moderator (referee) use?*
   Did it seem to work?

6. *What changes in the behavior of the two parties was necessary if the intervention and follow-up of this conflict was to have good results?*

7. *What cultural factors entered into this conflict and the way it was managed?*

8. *Any suggestions for improving the way this conflict was dealt with?*

Last year one of my colleagues and I were in the Philippines to speak in a field conference and also to intervene in a growing problem there. The national church has been going through the "independence" stage. Many of the national leaders are younger and well-trained men who want to call the shots in the work. Missionaries are to say "yes" when told where and how to serve within the country.

Our missionaries expressed to us that they felt they had little or nothing to say about the direction of the work or about their placement and ministries. Some were facing role dilemma – a feeling of having little influence and of not having fulfilling ministries to carry on. Recently out of frustration one young couple had left the field and now another experienced couple – Ray and Susan – were thinking of doing the same if their situation could not be changed. Their specific frustration was that they had been appointed by the national church leadership to work in our local church in Santiago, under a national pastor. But they had little meaningful ministry in the church. They felt that all they were contributing was their presence and tithes. They wanted to be released to start a new church in a new sector of the city. The national pastor wanted them to continue in his church as they had been doing. We feared losing this couple.

Our strategy was to first meet separately with the missionary couple just mentioned (Ray and Susan), then with the pastor of the church in Santiago where Ray and Susan were serving, and finally with the main national leaders. We discussed Ray and Susan's situation, asked for possible solutions to their immediate problem, and used this as a springboard to address the larger issue of a healthier and more equitable partnership relationship between the national church and the missionaries.

When the parties mentioned above all met together with us later, we asked for possible options for Ray and Susan. One was for them to continue in the church but with a broader ministry. The other was for them to be appointed to start a new church in a completely different area of Santiago. The nationals began to realize that if Ray and Susan continued in the same situation they might end up leaving the Philippines. No decision was made at that time, though it was later agreed that they be freed to start a new church, while continuing to be available to help the present established church when needed for advice and for preaching and teaching.

We then addressed the larger issue of a more equitable and healthy relationship between church leaders and missionaries. Here we asked the nationals to put themselves in the missionaries' shoes and we asked them whether they would be willing to assume the kind of role that Ray and Susan had been given – a largely passive, presence role. Several of the pastors agreed that they would need to have a much fuller ministry to be satisfied and challenged. We asked if it would not be better for all parties if we moved to an interdependent, partnership model where together we would decide on the placement and ministries of missionaries.

The negotiation and discussion did not lead to a formal agreement while we were still in the Philippines. But feedback from the field indicates that the national church leaders have a better understanding of our missionaries' aspirations, goals, and feelings. They are more open to shifting from a "church-over-the-missionaries" relationship to a partnership relationship. We have lost no missionaries since then and the church and ministries are moving forward. There is, however, more negotiation needed to arrive at a mutual understanding and acceptance of an interdependent relationship. Progress has been made but now follow-up work needs to be done.

In our discussions with the national leaders we were courteous and calm throughout our discussions, but firm and specific. We felt that we had to get through to the national leaders regarding what was happening to our missionaries and reasons for it. We felt that they did get a new understanding and empathy for our missionaries' situation and that they began to see the need for a change in the relationship.

Questions:

1. *What was the immediate issue causing the conflict?*

   What was the deeper and broader issue causing the conflict?

2. *What would have been the likely consequences if the conflict issues were not dealt with and resolved?*

3. *What conflict management styles were used in dealing with the conflict? List two and explain your choices.*

4. *What were some of the positive approaches used in the process of dealing with this conflict?*

5. *What cultural factors may have played a part in this conflict?*

6. *What would you suggest for effective follow-up with the national church leaders in order to establish and confirm a new partnership relationship?*

REFERENCES

BOOKS

Arensberg, Conrad M., and Arthur Niehoff. *Introducing Social Change: A Manual for Americans Overseas*. Chicago: Aldine Publishing, 1964.

Augsberger, David. *Caring Enough to Confront*. Ventura, CA: Regal Books, 1981.

Blubaugh, J. A., and D. Pennington. *Communicating Across Differences*. Columbus, OH: Charles E. Merrill Publishing, 1976.

Casse, Pierre, and S. Doel. *Managing Intercultural Negotiations: Guidelines for Trainers and Negotiators*. Washington, D.C.: SIETAR International, 1985.

Dale, Robert D. *Ministers as Leaders*. Nashville: Broadman Press, 1984.

Davis, S. M. *Comparative Management: Organizational and Cultural Perspectives*. Englewood Cliffs, NJ: Prentice Hall, 1971.

Dow, Robert Arthur. *Learning Through Encounter*. Valley Forge, PA: Judson Press, 1971.

Fisher, Glen. *International Negotiation: A Cross-Cultural Perspective*. Chicago: Intercultural Press, 1980.

Fisher, Roger, and William Ury. *Getting to Yes: Negotiating Agreement Without Giving In*. New York: Penguin Books, 1981.

Flynn, Leslie B. *Great Church Fights*. Wheaton, IL: Victor Books, 1976.

Foster, George M. *Traditional Cultures: And the Impact of Technological Change*. New York: Harper and Row, 1962.

Ford, Leroy. *Design for Teaching and Training: A Self-Study Guide to Lesson Planning*. Nashville: Broadman Press, 1978.

Hall, Edward T. *The Silent Language*. Garden City, NY: Anchor Press,/Doubleday, 1973.

Hersey, Paul, and Kenneth Blanchard. *Management of Organizational Behavior: Utilizing Human Resources*. Englewood Cliffs, NJ: Prentice Hall, 1977.

Hesselgrave, David J. *Communicating Christ Cross-Culturally*. Grand Rapids, MI: Zondervan, 1978.

Huggett, Joyce. *Creative Conflict*. Downers Grove, IL: Inter-Varsity Press, 1984.

Johnson, David W. *Human Relations and Your Career*. Englewood Cliffs, NJ: Prentice Hall, 1978.

Leas, Speed. *Laymen's Guide to Conflict Management*. Washington, D.C.: The Alban Institute, 1979.

_____. *Leadership and Conflict*. Nashville: Abingdon Press, 1982.

_____. *Should the Pastor be Fired*. Washington, D.C.: The Alban Institute, 1980.

Leas, Speed, and Paul Kittlaus. *Church Fights: Managing Conflict in the Local Church*. Philadelphia: Westminster Press, 1973.

McSwain, Larry L., and William C. Treadwell, Jr. *Conflict Ministry in the Church*. Nashville: Broadman Press, 1981.

Moore, Christopher W. *The Mediation Process: Practical Strategies for Resolving Conflict*. San Francisco: Jossey-Bass, 1986.

Moran, R. T., and R. P. Harris. *Managing Cultural Differences*. Houston: Gulf Publishing, 1979.

Oliver, Robert T. *Culture and Communication*. Springfield, IL: Charles C. Thomas Publisher, 1962.

Perry, Lloyd M., and Gilbert A. Peterson. *Churches in Crisis*. Chicago: Moody Press, 1977.

Perry, Lloyd M. *Getting the Church on Target*. Chicago: Moody Press, 1977.

Roth, Arnold. *Learning to Work Together*. Scottdale, PA: Herald Press, 1967.

Rush, Myron. *Management: A Biblical Approach*. Wheaton, IL: Victor Books, 1983.

Shawchuck, Norman. *How to Manage Conflict in the Church*. Schaumburg, IL: Spiritual Growth Resources, 1983.

Smedes, Lewis. *Forgive and Forget*. New York: Harper and Row, 1984.

Stagner, Ross (compiler). *The Dimensions of Human Conflict*. Detroit: Wayne State University Press, 1967.

This, Leslie E. *A Guide to Effective Management*. Reading, MA: Addison-Wesley, 1974.

Walton, Richard E. *Interpersonal Peacemaking: Confrontations and Third Party Consultations*. Reading, MA: Addison-Wesley, 1969.

ARTICLES

Ejigu, A. M. "Participative Management in a Developing Economy: Poison or Placebo?" *Journal of Applied Behavioral Sciences* 19, no. 3 (1983): 239-47.

Gish, Dorothy. "Sources of Missionary Stress." *Journal of Psychology and Theology* 11 (Fall 1983): 236-242.

Hefly, James C. "When There's a Conflict in Your Church." *Moody Monthly*, June 1987, 17-19.

Mann, Leon. "Cross-Cultural Studies of Small Groups." In *Handbook of Cross-Cultural Psychology: Social Psychology*, Vol. 5, by H. C. Triandis and R. W. Brislin, 155-209. Boston: Allyn and Bacon, 1980.

Morgan, Elisa. "How to Fight Right." *Focal Point*, January/March 1989, 3-4.

Segall, M. H. "Cognition: Information Processing in Various Cultures." In *Human Behavior in Global Perspective*, 96-135. Belmont, CA: Wordsworth, 1981.

_____. "Cultural Differences in Motives, Beliefs, and Values." In *Cross Cultural Psychology: Human Behavior in Global Perspective*, 136-79. Belmont, CA: Wordsworth, 1981.

Stogdill, R. M., and B. M. Bass. "Leadership in Different Cultures."
    In *Stogdill's Handbook of Leadership*, 522-49. New York:
    The Free Press, 1981.

UNPUBLISHED MATERIAL

Benson, Warren, and Mark H. Senter, III. "Church Management."
    Printed Notes for DMN course in Church Management,
    Trinity Evangelical Divinity School, Deerfield, IL,
    January 1988.

Mitchell, David J. "A Training Program for Conflict Management for
    Missionaries Entering or Engaged in Cross-Cultural
    Christian Ministry." DMN project for Conflict
    Management course, Trinity Evangelical Divinity School,
    Deerfield, IL, September 1986.

Vreugdenhill, Marion J. "Managing Conflict in the Church:
    Programmed Instruction." DMN project for Conflict
    Management course, Trinity Evangelical Divinity School,
    Deerfield, IL, July 1986.

HD 30.29 .P35 1990
Palmer, Donald C.
Managing conflict creatively

HD 30.29 .P35 1990
Palmer, Donald C.
Managing conflict creatively